Generations of Resistance

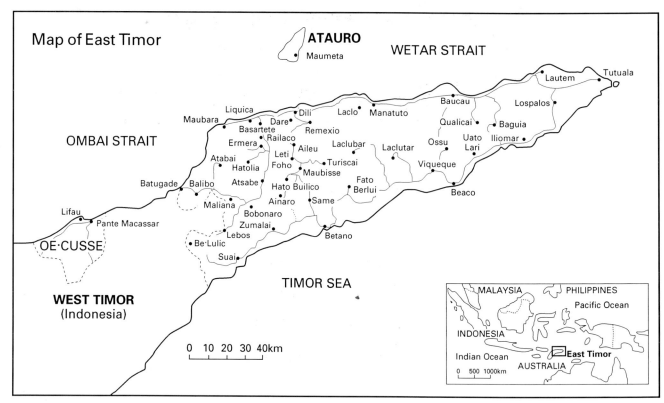

Map of East Timor

ATAURO
Maumeta

WETAR STRAIT

OMBAI STRAIT

Tutuala
Lautem
Baucau
Lospalos
Liquica
Dili
Laclo
Manatuto
Qualicai
Baguia
Maubara
Dare
Remexio
Ossu
Iliomar
Basartete
Uato
Ermera
Railaco
Aileu
Laclubar
Lari
Atabai
Leti
Laclutar
Viqueque
Hatolia
Foho
Turiscai
Atsabe
Maubisse
Batugade
Balibo
Hato Builico
Fato
Ainaro
Same
Berlui
Beaco
Maliana
Bobonaro
Betano
Lifau
Zumalai
Pante Macassar
Lebos
OE·CUSSE
Be·Lulic
Suai

WEST TIMOR
(Indonesia)

TIMOR SEA

0 10 20 30 40km

MALAYSIA   PHILIPPINES
                Pacific Ocean
INDONESIA
Indian Ocean   East Timor
              0 500 1000km   AUSTRALIA

Drawn by Ben Cracknell

Generations of Resistance

East Timor

Photographs by
STEVE COX

Historical introduction by
PETER CAREY

CASSELL

Cassell
Wellington House
125 Strand, London, WC2R 0BB

215 Park Avenue South
New York, NY 10003

First published 1995

British Library Cataloguing-in-Publication Data
A catalogue record for this book is available from the British Library

ISBN 0-304-33250-X (Hb)
0-304-33252-6 (Pb)

Designed and typeset by Ronald Clark

Printed at The University Press, Cambridge

Contents

Dedication

'The moment that will always live with me was in the chapel
in Santa Cruz cemetery and, feeling the gentle tug on my shirt
sleeve from behind me where piles of children were shielding
each other from the advancing soldiers, turning to find the out-
stretched arm of a little girl trying to force a smile while holding
the camera lens that had fallen out of my bag'

This book is for that little girl and the courage of all the
Timorese people in their fight for freedom.

Foreword

In East Timor the crosses are almost everywhere: great black crosses etched against the sky, crosses on peaks, crosses in tiers on the hillsides, crosses beside the road overlooking white slabs. They litter the earth and crowd the eye. Walk into the scrub and they are there, on the edge, a riverbank, an escarpment, commanding all before them. The inscriptions on some are normal: those of generations departed in proper time and sequence. But look at the dates of these and you see they are all prior to 1975, when proper time and sequence ended. Look at the dates on most of them and they reveal the extinction of whole families, wiped out in the space of a year, a month, a day. 'R.I.P. Mendonca, Crismina, 7.6.77 . . . Mendonca, Filismina, 7.6.77 . . . Mendonca, Adalino, 7.6.77 . . . Mendonca, Alisa, 7.6.77 . . . Mendonca, Rosa, 7.6.77 . . .'

More than 200,000 people, or a third of the East Timorese population, died as a direct result of the Indonesian invasion in 1975; and people are still dying under a brutal and illegal occupation that represents a crime against humanity in the strictist meaning of that term. We would not be aware of the full extent of this outrage were it not for a few brave people like the photographer Steve Cox. I first knew about the family listed above from a black-and-white photograph of Steve's that remained in my memory as stark evidence of what I would later see in East Timor. It was Steve's extraordinary photo-journalism that largely alerted the world to what had remained, effectively, a secret for sixteen years. When Indonesian troops massacred more than 270 young people in the Santa Cruz cemetery in Dili, the East Timorese capital, Steve was a crucial witness who, although fearing for his own life, took photographs that are a tribute to his subjects and to him. Look carefully at the image of four young men taken in the immediate aftermath of the Santa Cruz massacre; the two who are wounded, one of them seriously, are being cared for by the other two. And look at the image of the boy in his early teens, defiant in front of a banner depicting the resistance leader, Xanana Gusmão. This boy was later shot dead in the cemetery. Together they are a microcosm of the East Timorese struggle, and tell us why the Indonesian tyranny has failed to defeat such a people.

In the context, Steve Cox is a dangerous man. His work represents a threat not only to the perpetrators of the crime in East Timor but to those who, at a respectable distance, are complicit. When Steve flew into Darwin from Timor, following the massacre, he was the only passenger to be body-searched by Australian officials. 'It was clear they had been tipped off by the Indonesians and were looking for my film,' he said. 'They were disappointed because I had given it to another passenger, who hid it.'

Steve's photographs strip away the veils of hypocrisy that cover the complicity of governments, such as those of Australia and Britain. Shortly before the Santa Cruz massacre, Britain's Foreign Secretary Douglas Hurd urged his European colleagues to 'cut aid to countries that violate human rights'. Shortly after the massacre, the British government increased its aid to the Suharto dictatorship by 250 per cent to £81 million. Within weeks of Hurd's visit to Jakarta, to dispense this 'aid', the British government announced it had 'successfully negotiated' the sale to Indonesia of Hawk ground-attack 'training' aircraft made by British Aerospace. Eye witnesses have described Hawks attacking East Timorese villages. Today, Britain is Indonesia's biggest arms supplier. In addition to Hawks, British manufacturers have supplied helicopters, missiles, tanks, frigates, battlefield communications systems and a fully equipped Institute of Technology for the Indonesian armed forces. 'The Indonesian military,' states Amnesty International, 'has always been organized to deal with domestic rather than international threats.' East Timor is given as an example of such a 'threat'.

The secret is out now. East Timor is a cause for grave concern throughout the world and is firmly on an international human rights agenda that denies repectability to the generals in Jakarta. It is difficult to know where this will lead; but I have little doubt that the people of East Timor, like the peoples of South Africa, and Namibia and Eritrea, will eventually gain their freedom; and the photo-journalism collected in this fine book will have played no small part.

John Pilger

Introduction

In a century which has been marked by more bloodshed, pain and human violence than any in recorded history, the case of East Timor is unique both in the intensity of its suffering and in the reluctance of the international community to recognize what has come to pass during the last twenty years (1975–95): at least a third of the pre-1975 population murdered by the Indonesian army or perished as the result of war-induced famine and disease and a continuing military occupation as oppressive as any witnessed in post-war history – the slow death of a society and a culture. In brief, a form of ethnocide designed to undermine local values and replace them with an alien 'Indonesian-ness', the national values of a Muslim Javanese colonial power.

In 1995, our television screens are full of events in Bosnia, the Caucasus (Chechenia) and the Middle East. Yet had it not been for the courage and persistence of photographers like Steve Cox and film-makers like Max Stahl, who captured the horror of the November 1991 Santa Cruz massacre, would we today have any true sense of the reality of existence in what was once Timor Leste? It is a sad fact that there is now a pornography of perception just as much as there is a pornography of power. This is dictated almost exclusively by the international media. No CNN, no story – no TV pictures, no popular awareness – will stand as an epitaph of our age.

This is why this book is so important. By presenting these startling images of everyday life in East Timor under Indonesian occupation, Steve Cox has enabled us to get beyond the glib mendacity of government press releases and the fleeting reports of foreign journalists, heavily constrained as they are by the ubiquitous surveillance of the Indonesian/Timorese *bufo* (spies) and their military minders. Steve did this by spending as much time as possible with ordinary Timorese both in Dili and in the mountainous interior, and by travelling on an aged motorbike throughout the island. By gaining the trust of the local inhabitants – his fluent Portuguese stood him in good stead here – and by his frank and sympathetic manner, he was able to establish an unusual rapport with the Timorese population. Long years of colonial rule, the brutalities of the Japanese (1942–45) and, more recently (post-1975), the Javanese/Indonesians, have honed in the Timorese a deep perceptiveness, the penetrating gaze of those who live from day to day with suffering and death. It is this quality which he has captured in his photographs, a quality which George Orwell described in his great novel *Homage to Catalonia* (1938) and his ringing assertion that 'no bomb that ever burst could shatter the crystal spirit!'.

What then of East Timor's future? Will it one day, like Eritrea and Namibia before it, take its rightful place in the community of nations? The answer is undoubtedly yes! The price of continued occupation – both material and political (not to speak of moral) – for Indonesia will ultimately prove too high. East Timor's modern colonial bondage has been a direct result of the Cold War, of an international 'order' which condemned Vietnam to nearly three decades of war, which sealed the fate of over half a million Indonesian 'Communists' in the aftermath of the failed 'coup' of 30 September 1965, and which made the conditions possible for the 'auto-genocide' of the Khmer Rouge in Cambodia

(1975–78). The regime of President Suharto since 1966, with its unfettered authoritarianism and dominance of the military, was for long a direct beneficiary of the politics of the Cold War. Indeed, so delighted were the Americans at the overthrow of the populist President Sukarno in 1965–66 and the destruction of the Indonesian Communist Party (PKI) – at that time the largest in the non-communist world – that successive US administrations were prepared to look with excessive indulgence on Suharto and the Indonesian generals. 'He may be a son-of-a-bitch, but he's *our* son-of-a-bitch', as President Franklin Delano Roosevelt once said of a particularly offensive Central American dictator (Anastasio Somoza of Nicaragua), encapsulated American attitudes towards Indonesia throughout the majority of Suharto's 'New Order' (1967 to present).

This international context is important to bear in mind when considering the savagery of the Indonesian onslaught on East Timor in 1975. Frustrated by the victory of the leftist *Frente Revolucionária de Timor Leste Independente* (Fretilin) in the three-week civil war (11 August to early September 1975) against its centrist UDT (*União Democrática Timorense*) opponents in securing a political takeover of the former Portuguese territory, something which Suharto's intelligence chief, Ali Moertopo, had abortively schemed to achieve through his sinisterly named '*Operasi Komodo*' (Operation Komodo), the Indonesian military was given the green light for a full-scale invasion. Throughout the autumn months of 1975 (September to November), the military pressure on the short-lived Fretilin government in Dili grew relentlessly, with Indonesian warships shelling the coast and elite units of the Indonesian army striking ever deeper across the East Timor frontier.

The executions of five Western journalists (two Australians, two Britons and a New Zealander) at the border town of Balibo in mid-October 1975 highlighted the lengths to which the Indonesians were prepared to go to cover their tracks and prevent news of their actions reaching the West. Western intelligence – especially the Australian Defense Department and the CIA – obliged; up-to-date knowledge, based on careful monitoring of Indonesian signals traffic, was suppressed in the interests of good relations with Indonesia. 'If it comes to a crunch and there is a row in the UN, we should keep our heads down and avoid siding against the Indonesian Government', the words of a senior British Ambassador in Jakarta in July 1975 were echoed by the American Ambassador to Jakarta, who hoped that if the Indonesians did invade East Timor they would do so 'effectively, quickly and not use our equipment'. This was the year of the communist victories in Indochina and the collapse of the US-backed regimes in Phnom Penh and Saigon. With vital strategic interests at stake in Southeast Asia – not least the security of its deepwater SSBN nuclear submarine lanes through the Ombai-Wetar straits just off East Timor's northern coast – this was not a time for Washington and its Western allies to be contemplating the creation of a new left-leaning mini-state – a Southeast Asian Cuba as some pretended in Jakarta – adjacent to Indonesia's desperately underdeveloped and vulnerable eastern flank. The fact that the long-expected Indonesian invasion (7 December 1975) occurred just a day after President Gerald Ford and Secretary of State Henry Kissinger's brief official visit to Jakarta, merely confirmed what had long been suspected – the West's collusion with Indonesia's policy of armed annexation.

What had not been foreseen was the sheer incompetence and inadequacy of the Indonesian forces to the task in hand. 'We shall have breakfast in Dili, lunch in Baucau and dinner in Lospalos' had been the proud boast of General Benny Murdani, the officer in charge of the Indonesian operation, yet it took the best part of three years (1975–78) for the Indonesians to begin to consolidate their hold on the interior with the capture of the Mount Matebian redoubt in the eastern zone (22 November 1978) and the death of the Fretilin leader, Nicolau Lobato (31 December 1978). Estimates of Indonesian losses during this period run as high as two army divisions (16,000), a staggering figure considering that the total number of Fretilin fighters was never more than about 20,000. But high as the level of Indonesian casualties was, it was totally eclipsed by the ten times as many East Timorese civilians who perished. Why were mortality rates so astronomical? The sheer intensity of the fighting, the forced displacements of population by the Indonesians, and the widespread famine which followed the encirclement operations of 1978–79, are all certainly important here. Yet, there were other elements which heightened the savagery of the conflict. First, it is clear that when the Indonesian army commenced its operations against East Timor in 1975, soldiers were briefed by their officers that the East Timorese resistance was 'Communist' and that elements of both the North Sulawesi Permesta (*Perjuangan Alam Semesta*) federalist revolt (1958–61) and the once massive Indonesian Communist Party (PKI) had taken refuge there and were coordinating the resistance. Given the intensity of the bloodletting in Indonesia after 1965, and the collective hysteria generated by the army orchestrated anti-communist witch-hunt, it is hardly surprising that the military campaign had such devastating effects on the local population, especially when it became clear that Fretilin enjoyed widespread popular support. 'When you clean your field, don't you kill all the snakes, the small and large alike?' was the response of one Indonesian soldier when asked by a foreign journalist why the army was also massacring young children. In this fashion, the East Timorese population were subjected to a particularly vicious form of 'total war', which created, in the territory's narrow island confines, what the French author, Bernard Fall, referring to another conflict (the 1954 Vietnamese onslaught on the French garrison at Dien Bien Phu), once called 'hell in a very small place'.

The willingness of Western governments to provide the Indonesians with state-of-the-art weaponry, particularly war-planes adapted to counter-insurgency operations, was also crucial here. It is no coincidence that just as military analysts were reporting that the Indonesians were rapidly 'running out of inventory [ie armaments]', Western governments stepped forward to make good these losses. Thus the Jimmy Carter 'Human Rights' Administration (1977–81) provided Jakarta with 13 OV-10F 'Bronco' aircraft from the Rockwell International Corporation in February 1977 with the aid of an official US Government foreign military sales credit, and 16 McDonnell-Douglas A-4E 'Skyhawk' counter-insurgency bombers in August 1978, planes which were used with devastating effect to drop cluster bombs, napalm and chemical defoliants against the civilian populations sheltering in the Mount Matebian range. Survivors of those terrible onslaughts speak of scenes reminiscent of Dante's *Inferno* as whole communities were incinerated alive. Today, the British have replaced the Americans as the main armourer of the Suharto regime, and they are currently busy re-equipping their airforce with a new generation of the most modern British Aerospace 'Hawk' ground attack aircraft to replace its ageing Skyhawks.

Faced with the *realpolitik* of the international arms industry and the seemingly inexorable pressure of the Indonesians on the indigenous East Timorese through the steady influx of migrants from inner Indonesia (who now constitute a fifth of the total population of 750,000), the use of the Indonesian language (*Bahasa*) in all schools, and the commercial dominance of the non-native sectors of the population, what hope is there for the people of East Timor? The arrest (November 1992), trial (March 1993) and imprisonment of the locally revered East Timorese resistance leader, Xanana Gusmão, and some of his key lieutenants, the vicious reprisals conducted by the Indonesian army after the Santa Cruz massacre (12 November 1991) against the student activists, and the increasing constraints on the Catholic Church, would all seem to indicate that the days of the East Timorese resistance are numbered. Yet, just as Indonesian repression has been intensifying, so changes have been occurring within Indonesia and in the new post-Cold War international order which may spell new hope for East Timor. In Indonesia itself, opposition to the rule of the 74-year-old Suharto is growing, and there is a realization that major changes, perhaps including a move towards more democratic political forms, will be essential if the Republic is to continue to develop in the twenty-first century in ways which will guarantee jobs for its ever-swelling labour force.

At the same time, internationally, there is now a greater willingness to criticize Indonesia's human rights record – as witnessed by the Indonesian defeat in the UN Human Rights Commission in March 1993 when the US joined with its Western allies to ensure support for a European Union motion highly critical of Jakarta's record in East Timor – and the decision on the part of some countries to link progress in the human rights field to economic issues: Indonesia's GSP (Generalized System of Preferential Tariffs) privileges are currently under review in Washington. Paradoxically, Indonesia's very success in securing the arrest of Xanana has led to greater international awareness of the East Timor situation. The blatant illegality of his 'trial', the heavy-handed treatment of witnesses, and the recent public relations disaster of the APEC (Asia-Pacific Economic Conference) summit in Jakarta (14–15 November 1994), when 29 East Timorese students and workers staged a public protest at the US Embassy in Jakarta, have all drawn attention to the wider illegality of Indonesia's 20-year occupation. Much in the same fashion as Dutch colonial rule in Indonesia in the 1930s was entering its final phase even as it seemed to have silenced all the main Indonesian nationalist leaders, so Jakarta's latter-day colonialism in East Timor is being unravelled by the tide of contemporary events. In the last decade of the twentieth century, amid the preparation for the festivities to mark the fiftieth anniversary of the birth of the Indonesian Republic (17 August 1945), Jakarta may at last be realizing that colonialism, even in the ex-colonial Third World, tends to create its own gravediggers.

Peter Carey
Dzoghen Beara
West Cork, Ireland
January 1995

Historical background

When, in July 1976, Jakarta sought to 'legalize' its incorporation of East Timor as its 27th Province, it did so on the basis of a piece of political theatre: the acceptance by Suharto and the Indonesian Parliament (*Dewan Perwakilan Rakyat*) of a 'petition' from a hastily arranged 'People's Representative Council of the Region of East Timor' in Dili (convened *manu militari* by the Indonesian army) calling for full integration into Indonesia. Lacking any claim in international law to the former Portuguese territory, Jakarta propagated the convenient myth that it had been 'invited' into East Timor by leaders of the tiny pro-integrationist Apodeti (*Associacão Social Democrática Timorense*) party, UDT and others, on the basis of 'popular demand' and 'age-old ties of blood brotherhood' which 450 years of Portuguese colonialism had sundered. Had not Timor been part of the great East Javanese empire of Majapahit during its fourteenth-century heyday? Was it not time for those primordial relations, relations which long antedated the coming of the Europeans, to be reestablished? Was not blood thicker than the waters of the Ombai-Wetar straits, thicker than the fiat of colonial boundaries?

A glance at the map of Eastern Indonesia would seem to add credence to these arguments. Was it not an absurdity for the island of Timor, a mere 32,300 square kilometres (the same size as The Netherlands), to be divided down the middle, an arbitrary division arranged for the convenience of two colonial powers – the Portuguese and the Dutch – brokered by the International Court of Justice in 1914? What possible reason was there, other than the mere quirk of history, for the eastern part (together with the small western enclave of Oecussi-Ambeno) to be given to Portugal, and the western part to Holland?

When one turns to the ethno-linguistic map of Timor, however, this same, seemingly arbitrary, divide, does have some logic. Here, amid the myriad of smaller linguistic and ethnic groups, one can discern two principle ethnic populations: the Atoni, 'the people of the dry lands', estimated at some 400,000 in 1975, who inhabit the mountains at the centre of the island and what is now West Timor, and the Belu, subsequent invaders, who arrived between 3000 and 200 BC from the west (possibly South Sulawesi [Makasar] or the island of Ceram in the Moluccas, hence the origin myth of the island as a wandering crocodile from Makasar later turned to stone) and vanquished the less warlike Atoni, settling mainly in the eastern part. More racially mixed than the Atoni with traces of Malay, Melanesian and Austronesian blood, the Belu have long shared Tetun as a lingua franca, a language now spoken by nearly all the inhabitants of East Timor, including the populations of Papuan origin (Fatuluku; Maku'a) in the extreme eastern tip (Ponta Leste).

Throughout their period of historical supremacy, they also gained a reputation for their vigour and enterprise, particularly with regard to their use of economic resources. Their extreme mobility in the pursuit of trade and the development of mountain – swidden – agriculture based on scattered settlements was especially noticeable. Indeed, so struck were historical observers of colonial Timor by these characteristics, that the Belu and Atoni were often referred to as two 'distinct peoples', something which the Australian commandos who fought in Timor against the Japanese in 1942–43 also found: they made no headway in West Timor where the inhabitants were reluctant to offer assistance, but received unstinting support from the populations in the east. If one adds to this the very different historical experiences of the two halves of the island under Portuguese and Dutch rule respectively, then the distinctiveness of the peoples of East Timor is thrown into even sharper relief.

Unlike the Dutch, the Portuguese did not establish administrative structures which wrought deep-seated changes in traditional society. From the discovery of Timor by the Portuguese in 1514 – the island was renowned for its sandalwood – until the late nineteenth century, the Portuguese exercised what influence they could through the local rulers (*liurai rei*) and chieftains (*liurai*). Indeed, for long periods, Portuguese authority was represented not by crown-appointed colonial officials, but by Dominican missionaries and powerful *mestiço* (part-Portuguese, part-Timorese) families, known as the 'Black Portuguese' or 'Topasses' (from the Dravidian *'tupasse'* meaning an 'interpreter'). Even when the Portuguese did start to introduce a regular system of taxes in 1906, alongside the existing labour services for the production of coffee (1899), Timor's principal cash crop and source of profit for the colonial exchequer, the power of the *liurai* was little affected. Thus right up to the time of the Indonesian invasion in 1975, traditional social and political structures remained virtually intact in East Timor with local level administrators (*chefes de suco; povoação*) still drawing strength from their family and clan connections.

The Portuguese certainly did not develop Timor or educate its people – by the beginning of the 1970s, a mere 10 per cent (65,000) of the population were literate, and a still smaller proportion (0.25 per cent) had benefited from a Portuguese-language secondary and tertiary education which gave them the right to *assimilado / civilizado* ('assimilated' or 'civilized') status. Infrastructure was poor (there were only 30 kilometres of asphalt road in the colony) and there was only one doctor for every 27,000 inhabitants, one of the worst ratios in the whole Portuguese colonial world. But, despite this legacy, the Portuguese did give the population one great boon whose benefits were to become ever more obvious after the 1975 Indonesian invasion – they left them largely alone. They thus ensured the continuity of social and religious customs (by the mid-70s, there were still only about 220,000 Catholics in a population of around 680,000), and a certain stability of life rooted in the deep bonds of kinship and locality.

Unlike the populations of post-1945 Indonesia, who went through the bonding experience of the four-year struggle (1945–49) against the Dutch and the political vicissitudes of the independent republic under the charismatic but ill-starred President Sukarno (1945–66), the people of East Timor continued to live in a form of time warp. The modern world had passed them by, but the protection afforded by a declining colonial power was not without its benefits. With the population growing rapidly (2.2 per cent per annum) in the early 1970s, and Portugal beginning to take stock of its responsibilities (ambitious infrastructural schemes for East Timor, involving the construction of 400 kilometres of asphalt roads and five new airports, were being contemplated in the context of the fourth Portuguese five-year development plan [1974–78]), it might have seemed that the Timorese could look forward to a brighter future. They had reckoned without Suharto's 'New Order' and the savagery of his army.

Political awakening (1974–75)

The 'Carnation Revolution' of April 1974 which toppled the Caetano regime, successor to the forty-year dictatorship of Dr Antonio Salazar (1928–68), took most people unaware. Nowhere more so than in East Timor itself where the mildly reformist Governor, Colonel Alves Aldeia, had been incautious enough to denounce publicly the Portuguese Armed Forces Movement (*Movimento das Forças Armadas*) for its criticism of the Lisbon regime only days before it threw its armour against the presidential palace. The revolution ushered in two years of great political upheaval in Portugal, a country long isolated from the European mainstream, which witnessed the re-emergence of the pro-Moscow Portuguese Communist Party of Álvaro Cunhal, and a series of violent political swings which were only brought to an end by the April 1976 legislative elections and the emergence of Mário Soares (post-March 1986, President of Portugal) and his Socialist Party. These two years were to spell disaster for distant East Timor as the left-leaning administration of Colonel Vasco Gonçalves (in office, 1974–76) and President Costa Gomes sought ways to unburden themselves of the Timor problem through negotiations with Jakarta. After all, the Armed Forces Movement had been led by disgruntled army officers politicized by the disasters of the Portuguese colonial wars in Africa, which had cost the lives of 9,000 of their men and left 25,000 maimed. Decolonization was thus high on their agenda, and if a way could be found for Timor to be peacefully integrated with its vast Indonesian neighbour then so much the better.

The East Timorese, however, had other ideas: 'There would be no point in our joining with Indonesia after decolonization. Their side [ie West Timor and the Indonesian Province of Nusa Tenggara Timur] is poorer than ours, and instead of the Portuguese over us we would have the Javanese. This would be *re*colonization not decolonization!', the words of a Timorese interviewed in September 1974 by the former Australian consul in Dili, James Dunn, said it all. It was no secret to the East Timorese that most of the inhabitants of West Timor, including the energetic Governor, Brigadier-General El Tari, resented Java's Muslim military overlordship. Portuguese colonial officials, appalled by the political traumas of the mid-1960s in Indonesia, in particular Sukarno's West Irian campaign (1961–62), his 'Confrontation' with Malaysia (1962–66) and the bloody aftermath of the abortive 'Communist' coup of 30 September 1965, which had left over a million dead, had also not been slow to remind the East Timorese of the disasters which would befall the colony should Portugal be forced to depart.

It was thus hardly surprising that when political parties were finally allowed to be organized in East Timor in late April and early May 1974, the two largest – the right of centre UDT (*União Democrática Timorense*), and the more radical ASDT (*Assoçiação Social Democrática Timorense* [Association of Timorese Social Democrats]; post-September 1974, Fretilin) – were adamantly opposed to any notion of integration with Indonesia, the first looking for 'progressive autonomy' under the Portuguese flag, and the second for 'the [immediate] right to independence'. Only the tiny Apodeti (*Assoçiacão Popular Democrática Timorense;* Timorese Popular Democratic Association) party, was prepared to consider a merger with Indonesia, but even then this was to be conditional on a large measure of local autonomy (it was expected that East Timor would be allowed to govern itself and enjoy the same privileges as other Special Regions [*Daerah Istimewa*], such as Yogyakarta and Aceh, in the Indonesian Republic), and that it would take place 'in accordance with international law' (ie through a properly organized referendum) following a transitional period of one or two years in which the people of East Timor could get to know their Indonesian neighbours and learn their language (*Bahasa Indonesia*).

Developments in Dili were greeted with alarm in Jakarta. Political parties, free debate, the end of censorship, social democracy, independence, internationally-supervised referenda – these were all deeply threatening concepts for the Indonesian military. Had not the New Order Government and its '*pancasila* (the five principles of the Indonesian State) democracy' done away with the need for party politics? Anyway, had not the brief Indonesian experience with such politics in the early 1950s been a disaster? After the struggles to preserve the unitary Republic in the face of secessionist (Ambon, 1950) and federalist (Sumatra, 1957–58; North Sulawesi, 1958–61) revolts in the outer islands, what sort of precedent would an independent East Timor set, especially for the desperately under-developed provinces of eastern Indonesia? Would it not act as a magnet for Communist insurgency, thus jeopardizing everything that had been won at the cost of so much blood in the mid-1960s? No, an independent East Timor was unthinkable. It must be prevented at all costs!

If there was any doubt in the minds of Suharto's ministers – and Foreign Minister, Adam Malik, had been incautious enough to give the ASDT leader, José Ramos-Horta, a letter during his visit to Jakarta in June 1974, stating that 'the independence of every country is the right of every nation, with no exception for the people of Timor' – these were swept aside in the autumn of that year. This was the time when radical – Maoist-influenced – Timorese students started returning to Dili from Lisbon, and the ASDT party took a sharp turn to the left changing its name to Fretilin and embarking on a revolutionary social and economic reform programme (expropriation of large landholdings, inclusion of unused fertile land in a system of peasant co-operatives, participation of ordinary Timorese in local decision making, and adult literacy/educational policies), which owed much to the example of the successful liberation movements in Africa such as Amílcar Cabral's PAIGC (*Partido Africano da Independência da Guiné e Cabo Verde*) in Guinea-Bissau, and Frelimo (*Frente de Libertação de Moçambique*) in Mozambique, as well as Fr Paulo Freire's rural literacy/adult education programmes in Brazil.

In this very same month of September 1974, while ASDT was transforming itself into Fretilin, Suharto met with the Australian Prime Minister, Gough Whitlam, in the Central Javanese resort town of Wonosobo, and received an important endorsement for his integrationist Timor policy. 'An independent Timor would be an unviable state and a potential threat to the area', Whitlam is believed to have told his Indonesian host, adding, with somewhat less emphasis, 'that the wishes of the Timorese should be respected and that public reaction in Australia would be hostile if Indonesia used force'. In this fashion, Australia, the one country in the region which might have acted as a restraining influence on Jakarta, effectively sold the pass to the Indonesian generals. Talk of a 'voluntary union of Portuguese Timor with Indonesia, on the basis of an internationally acceptable act of self-determination, [which] would . . . serve the objective of decolonization and . . . the interests of stability in the region', as an Australian Government memo put it after the

Wonosobo meeting, was so much casuistry, given what was known in Canberra about the attitudes of most Timorese towards integration and Jakarta's woeful record on matters of self-determination, illustrated only five years earlier (1969) in the case of West Irian, when the former Dutch colony had been incorporated in the Republic by an 'act of free choice' consisting of the forcible extraction of votes from 1022 Irianese customary chiefs. In retrospect, Wonosobo was Timor's Munich, though another year was to elapse before its full implications became clear in Dili.

Build up to invasion (1975)

Now that Suharto had been assured of Australia's 'understanding' and the support of key Western countries such as the United States, concerned to protect its strategic interests (deepwater submarine passage through the Ombai-Wetar straits) at a time of heightened Cold War tension, and Japan, market for over 40 per cent of Indonesia's oil, he could begin to lay plans for East Timor's incorporation. Initially, it was hoped that this might be finessed through an intelligence operation master-minded by the President's long-serving intelligence supremo, Ali Moertopo (1924–84), and his cohort of Catholic Chinese advisers at Jakarta's Centre for Strategic and International Studies (CSIS). Their brain-child was the so-called *Operasi Komodo* (named after the giant lizard of the eponymous eastern Indonesian island), which was designed to manipulate the domestic political situation in Timor in such a way that a subsequent Indonesian intervention could be presented to the world as an 'invitation' from the Timorese leaders themselves to 'restore order' and ensure the 'successful integration' of the former Portuguese territory into the Republic.

In order to accomplish this, Moertopo and his advisers had first to crack a knotty problem. In January 1975, despite their differences of political emphasis, the two main Timorese pro-independence parties, UDT and Fretilin, had joined together in a coalition. As long as this held, Jakarta's chances of intervening successfully in East Timor were slight for it was obvious to all that the pro-integrationist Apodeti party commanded negligible popular support and presented few political prospects for the Indonesians. *Operasi Komodo*'s principle brief was thus to break this coalition, a task which it embarked on partly through the use of black propaganda against Fretilin 'Communists' beamed from its radio transmitter at Atambua on the Indonesian side of the Timor border, and partly through pressure on the UDT leadership. On various occasions in April and May 1975, these leaders travelled, expenses courtesy of CSIS, to Jakarta to meet with the intelligence chief and hear his concerns about their Fretilin coalition partners. At the same time, a Fretilin delegation was left in no doubt about Moertopo's intentions: Horta recalls how when asked what he would do with regard to developments in East Timor, Moertopo covered his face with his hand, splayed his fingers apart and said chillingly – 'we shall be watching you!'.

This combination of threats and warnings, playing as they did on existing tensions within the coalition, had the desired effect. At the end of May the UDT-Fretilin alliance split apart, and less than two weeks later (6 June 1975), Indonesian troops entered the Oecussi-Ambeno enclave, the part of East Timor surrounded by Indonesian territory, a sign that the Indonesian military was readying itself for direct intervention in East Timor itself. It was still hoped, however, that this intervention could be dressed up in some form of political 'legitimacy', and for this Moertopo had devised an even bolder scheme which involved plunging East Timor into civil war, and precipitating a situation in which Jakarta could be 'invited' to intervene to restore order. In July, the UDT leaders resumed their peregrinations to Jakarta, meeting Moertopo and other top Indonesian generals charged with the integration of the Portuguese colony. Events were now moving fast: on 17 July Constitutional Law 7/75 had been passed in Lisbon setting October 1976 as the date for popular elections for a General Assembly in East Timor to decide the territory's future, and October 1978 as the time for the final Portuguese withdrawal. Twelve days later, in elections for local councils – the only free elections ever held in East Timor – Fretilin candidates gained 55 per cent of the popular vote. Unless Moertopo and his UDT protégés acted with dispatch they might find that Fretilin had swept the board.

On 6 August, the UDT leaders returned to Dili and on 11 August, with the backing of the Dili Police Chief, Lieutenant-Colonel Rui Alberto Maggiolo Gouveia, they launched a coup designed to wrest power from the Portuguese and halt the growing popularity of Fretilin. Unfortunately, this stratagem completely backfired. Almost immediately, pro-Fretilin East Timorese troops in the Portuguese colonial army rallied to the party's support and just over a week later (19 August) had begun to retake Dili. By early September, the defeated UDT remnants were beginning to pour in disarray across the Indonesian border and by 24 September it was all over – Fretilin was in control of the whole of East Timor.

These dramatic events had significant consequences for all parties in East Timor, as well as for the Portuguese and the Indonesians. The involvement of East Timorese troops from the colonial army on the Fretilin side was a crucial development which not only ensured the party's victory over its opponents in the civil war, but also gave it a potent military capacity for the future: the *Forças Armadas de Libertação Nacional de Timor-Leste* (Falintil), Fretilin's military wing, formed on 20–21 August, could now draw on an elite corps of 2,500 professional troops, with a further 7,000 who had received military training under the Portuguese and another 10,000 who had attended courses of shorter duration. As a member of the North Atlantic Treaty Organization, Portugal's military forces were also equipped with the most up-to-date NATO weaponry including G3 automatic rifles, heavy calibre Mausers, bazookas, grenade launchers, mortars, light artillery pieces and Mercedes Unimog trucks for troop transport. Many of these weapons now fell into Fretilin hands when the recently re-equipped Portuguese arsenal and military base at Taibesse near Dili was captured in the early days of the fighting.

This combination of trained troops and modern equipment provided Fretilin with the military capacity to mount a highly effective resistance to the Indonesian cross-border incursions in the September–November period, and later to organize a co-ordinated campaign in the highland areas of East Timor which kept the Indonesians at bay for over three years (1975–78) following their 7 December 1975 invasion. It also brought to the fore gifted military leaders within Fretilin itself, men of the calibre of Nicolau Lobato (killed 31 December 1978), Hermenegildo Alves (Fretilin Vice-Minister of National Defense, killed 1978), Antonio Cavarinho (*alias* Mau Lear) (burnt alive after torture by the Indonesians, 2 February 1979), and José Alexandre (*alias* Xanana) Gusmão. Indeed, until the very changed circumstances of the mid- to late 1980s, when the student-led *intifada* began to have an influence on the development of the nationalist struggle in Timor, the military wing of Fretilin provided the critical component of its leadership.

For Fretilin's opponents, especially the UDT, the August–September civil war was a disaster. Once they had crossed the border into Indonesian West Timor, the UDT leaders found that they were little more than prisoners of the Indonesian military forced to do their bidding. Their 'petition' for the integration of East Timor into Indonesia, signed at Atambua under the barrels of Indonesian guns, on 7 September 1975, was later to provide the basis for the infamous 'Balibo' declaration – concocted in a Bali hotel, Moertopo giving instructions that the final two letters should be added to make it look more 'authentically' Timorese – which was formally ratified on 29 November (a day after the Fretilin declaration of East Timorese independence) by Indonesian Foreign Minister Adam Malik.

Although the civil war turned out very differently from what Moertopo had expected, it proved useful to Jakarta's propaganda service, especially when inconvenient questions began to be asked in the aftermath of the 7 December invasion. First, the Indonesians pretended that far from ending in a Fretilin victory in September, the civil war dragged on for months, years even. According to Jakarta, the Indonesian army did not 'invade' East Timor in December 1975, instead Dili was 'liberated from the Communist yoke' by forces made up of the UDT and Apodeti 'militias', 'backed up' by Indonesian 'volunteers'. The resultant deaths – even the Indonesians admitted to a high death toll (in April 1977, Adam Malik spoke of 'perhaps as many as 80,000' Timorese civilian casualties) – were thus not the responsibility of the Indonesian army, but the 'tragic consequence of the fratricidal struggle between the Timorese belligerents themselves'. The careful assessment by the International Committee of the Red Cross (ICRC), who had full access to the territory in September (something which they rarely enjoyed in the aftermath of the Indonesian invasion), that civil war deaths did not exceed 1,500, was simply ignored by the Indonesians.

Second, Jakarta could claim that the Portuguese 'abandoned their responsibilities' during the civil war when the Governor, Mário Lemos Pires (in office, November 1974–December 1975), his entire staff and 200-strong military force evacuated Dili for the adjacent island of Atauro (the aptly named 'Isle of Goats'). Certainly, the Portuguese withdrawal was inexcusable – they *had* abandoned ship – and the signals coming from Lisbon seemed to indicate that the Gonçalves Government would sorely like to be rid of the whole East Timor problem, but what the Indonesians conveniently omitted to mention was their own hand in the events which precipitated the civil war, and the wider destabilization of the colony.

Throughout September and October 1975, the Indonesian military build-up on the border continued. By mid-September the US Central Intelligence Agency (CIA) was reporting that 650 Indonesian troops – special forces (*Komando Pasukan Sandi Yudha/ Kopassandha*) under the command of Colonel (later General) Dading Kalbuadi and units of the Indonesian Army's Strategic Reserve (KOSTRAD) including a battalion of the crack West Java Siliwangi division – were fighting inside East Timor while Indonesian warships shelled the coast. On 6 October, these forces, backed by elements of the East Java Brawijaya Division and naval commandos (KKO), launched a full-scale assault on the border town of Batugadé which fell two days later. Despite the size of these operations, and the accuracy of Western intelligence monitoring, it was not in the interests of either the Indonesians or their Western backers to allow too much reporting of these developments in the Western media. Thus, when two Melbourne-based camera crews (two Australians, two Britons and a New Zealander) got too close to the fighting at the border town of Balibo on 16 October, and secured footage of the Indonesian attack, they were summarily executed by the KKO unit involved.

News of this event was suppressed by the Australian authorities, even though they were privy to the Defence Signals Division monitoring from Shoal Bay in Australia's Northern Territory. Reports of what had happened – that the 'newsmen had been machine-gunned and their bodies burnt' – were only to seep out later, and then *soto voce* through anonymous phone calls from troubled intelligence officials whose consciences momentarily outweighed their security pledges.

The official response to the incident from Canberra, as well as London and Wellington, was supine: What were Westerners doing there anyway? They should have stayed away from Timor and let the Indonesians resolve the problem in their own way! East Timor was bound to become a part of Indonesia – why should Western reporters create difficulties when trade and political contacts with Jakarta were *so* good? Again, the message to the East Timorese came over loud and clear – you are on your own! Make shift as best you can! Better still, accept the inevitable and go quietly into the Indonesian fold!

So the weeks passed with every day new pressures bearing down on the embattled Fretilin administration in Dili. The inspired rearguard action of Fernando Carmo (later killed in Dili on the first day of the Indonesian invasion in a doomed attempt to save the Australian reporter, Roger East) cost the Indonesians dear in the fighting for the fertile Maliana plain in October, but the sheer weight of Indonesian fire-power – from land, sea and air – wore the Timorese down. By mid-October Maliana had fallen, and by early November the Indonesians were massing for an attack along the Lois River with the aim of taking the stronghold at Atabae, one of the last defensive positions before Dili.

All this time, Fretilin convoys, heavily laden with arms, ammunition and food, ground up the steep roads to the south of the capital heading for carefully prepared bases in the central highlands from where the guerrilla struggle would be continued after the Indonesian invasion. On the political front, desperate attempts were made to bring the Portuguese back into negotiations, and appeals sent to the outside world to bring pressure to bear on Jakarta. All to no purpose: Portugal was too preoccupied with its own internal problems to give much thought to the fate of Timor (Governor Pires on distant Atauro waited in vain for replies to his telegrams). The West was too indifferent. Who cared about Timor? It was just another of those 'far-away countries about which we know nothing'. Thus Neville Chamberlain's spiritual descendants lived on in Western chanceries.

On 26 November Atabae fell. The road to Dili lay open. Two days later in a grim, brave little ceremony in Dili, the Fretilin President, Xavier do Amaral, was driven to the Portuguese colonial government's Administrative Palace in the Governor's Mercedes there to sign a declaration proclaiming:

Unilaterally, the independence of East Timor, from 00.00 hours today [28 November 1975], declaring the state of the Democratic Republic of East Timor, anti-colonialist and anti-imperialist.

Let us at least die with our boots on, citizens of an independent state, the Democratic Republic of Timor Leste! '*Pátria ou Morte!*' (Fatherland or Death!).

Invasion (7 December 1975)

While most Timorese knew that the Indonesians were plotting a major operation – only the previous February extensive military exercises had taken place in Lampung (Southern Sumatra) as a dry run for the amphibious assault on Dili, and *Operasi Komodo*'s radio station had been giving out warnings to foreign journalists to leave Dili – few could have guessed its scale, savagery and incompetence. By a sinister stroke of timing – dictated partly by the need not to embarrass the American President, Gerald Ford, and his Secretary of State, Henry Kissinger, during their two-day official visit to Jakarta (5–6 December) – the attack was launched on Sunday, 7 December, exactly 34 years to the day after the surprise Japanese attack on Pearl Harbour (1941). Involving some 10,000 troops (special forces, paratroops, Marines [*Korps Marinir*] and battalions drawn from the Siliwangi and Brawijaya Divisions), and codenamed *Operasi Seroja* ('Operation [Blossoming] Lotus'), it began with a naval bombardment of Fretilin positions east and west of the town. Then, just before dawn, paratroops began dropping into the waterfront area, near the prestigious Farol district, recently home to the departed Portuguese officials.

From the start, however, the operation was marred by poor co-ordination – it was apparently the largest amphibious operation ever attempted in Indonesia's post-independence history, and it cruelly exposed the deficiencies in the discipline, training, and equipment (70 per cent of all Indonesian mortar rounds were found to be duds) of Indonesia's crack units. Here was an army trained principally for domestic garrison duties and internal counter-insurgency – the crushing of small-scale federalist revolts in the outer islands, and the killing of unarmed civilians suspected of Communist sympathies in 1965–66 – now being thrown into battle against a disciplined foe, one intimately acquainted with his home territory and deeply imbued with the justice of his cause. As the Japanese found to their cost during the Second World War, when they had suffered over 1,500 casualties (out of a total occupying force of 20,000) at the hands of a 400-strong Australian commando force, Timor was superb guerrilla country, a death-trap for conventional armies.

So it proved for the Indonesians. Their total losses will never be known, but in the first four years of fighting in East Timor (1975–78), some estimate that they may have taken 16,000 casualties, equivalent to two Indonesian divisions. In a remarkable interview with a Jakarta journal in 1993, General Dading Kalbuadi, the first Indonesian military commander in East Timor after the invasion, admitted 'I feel really terrible, because more of my boys died than under any other [commander], and more wives were widowed . . . You know the Taman Seroja [Lotus Garden] housing complex [in Jakarta] [for disabled veterans of the East Timor war]? I don't have the courage to go there, because I feel such pity' (*Jakarta, Jakarta*, 24–30 July 1993, p.30). In fact, the Indonesian authorities did everything possible to hide the scale of the carnage from the Indonesian public, even refusing to allow wives to visit their husbands in the casualty wards of the principal military hospitals in Jakarta. Officially, Indonesia was not involved with the war in East Timor, the only Indonesians there being a few gallant 'volunteers' supporting the anti-Fretilin forces, a fiction sustained by removing the insignia indicating rank and unit from the uniforms of the invading troops.

Just how costly the fighting would be was clear from the start, and was compounded by the downright incompetence of the Indonesian general staff, especially the officers charged with planning and directing the operation. Some of the paratroops were dropped short and fell into the sea, drowning under the weight of their equipment, others were dropped on Fretilin forces withdrawing from the town, so they were unable to block off their retreat. After taking casualties, they then came under fire from Indonesian Marine units driving inland who mistook them for the enemy. Caught in this murderous crossfire, the discipline of the remaining paratroops broke down completely and they began a rampage through the town, killing and looting as they went.

They were not the only unit to turn their guns on the civilian population – hundreds of civilians (many of them Chinese) were shot down by the troops coming up from the waterfront area. In the first few days of the invasion, it is estimated that 2,000 Dili inhabitants (700 of them Chinese) died, a far worse death toll than anything experienced under the Japanese. Even Apodeti supporters, who had just been released from Fretilin internment, were machine-gunned in the streets when they went out to greet their 'liberators'. So much for the Indonesian Government's fiction of Dili's release from the 'Communist yoke' by the combined forces of the UDT and Apodeti 'militias'. In that day of carnage, they were nowhere to be seen. Instead, everywhere were the red, orange, green and violet berets of the Indonesian special forces, marines and Strategic Reserve (KOSTRAD) battalions, blood-bolstered vanguard of Indonesia's blitzkrieg.

Among the most macabre of the mass executions carried out in Dili occurred at the jetty where two groups of around 30 and 60 respectively – the first mainly women whose children were torn from them – were shot in the head at point-blank range, their bodies falling into the sea. With each execution, the Indonesians forced the crowd of 500 terrified onlookers to count aloud – one number for each victim. Among the victims was the Australian journalist, Roger East, who had been captured shortly after sending his last dispatches from the Marconi Centre on the morning of the invasion, and Nicolau Lobato's wife, Isabel, whose body was later found with a stake driven through her vagina. These killings, later known as the Aria Branca massacre (from the white sandy beach close to the Farol area, where the bodies were eventually washed up), were but the first of many which were to scar the twenty years of Indonesian occupation, years which were to see the death of perhaps as many as a third of the pre-1975 Timorese population of close on 700,000.

Besides the indiscriminate killings, the Indonesian invasion also brought in its train other forms of violence and destruction. One of the most notable was old-fashioned plunder. In their propaganda, the Indonesians often spoke about the restoration of age-old links of 'brotherhood' with the Timorese, links which date back to fourteenth-century Majapahit. In making these associations, one wonders if the Indonesians realized their deep irony – after all, Majapahit was an old-style empire based on trade, plunder and punitive expeditions, its influence being marked more by random violence – at least in the more far-flung islands of the Indonesian archipelago supposedly under its sway – than by any system of ordered administration. With the violent onslaught of the late twentieth-century Indonesian army on Timor's shores in 1975, the years seemed to fall away – Republican Indonesia and imperial Majapahit were as one. Here was history repeating itself with ghastly inevitability: the same imperial Java, the same tributary outer islands. The only thing that had changed was the destructiveness of the modern weaponry and the sheer scale of senseless devastation.

Thus, alongside the landing-craft, now rusting into the Dili sand, sinister reminders of that terrible December day, came other less warlike vessels – cargo ships from Java arriving to take away the contents of plundered houses and public buildings. To facilitate this process, the surviving residents of the capital were summoned to Dili airport, there to undergo a 'residency check'. During their absence, all objects of value were removed from their homes and from the Portuguese-built institutions: door frames, windows, refrigerators, radios, roofing material, furniture, operating theatres, Marconi radio transmitters, mirrors, copper pipes, bathroom fittings, vehicles and motor-cycles – in brief, anything portable (even bodies were later exhumed by collectors of gold teeth, and Timorese labour gangs conscripted to dig up the graves of Timorese *liurai*, many of whom had precious objects buried with them). Shipped immediately to Java, some of these items, like booty from the vanquished courts of colonial Indonesia, started turning up in hotel suites and generals' villas in Jakarta and Bali.

Material plunder had its counterpart in the raiding of the bodies of women and girls: female relatives of Fretilin fighters, and members of Fretilin-affiliated women's and student's organizations were particularly at risk. Many were arrested and imprisoned, some in a section of the Hotel Tropical in the centre of Dili, where they were subjected to torture – a favourite Indonesian method was the use of fierce burning *krétèk* (clove cigarettes) on breasts, faces and bare flesh. Many were raped repeatedly by their guards, and six months after the invasion over half were pregnant. The same pattern was repeated all over Timor in the villages and towns taken over by Indonesian troops where young women and girls (some barely in their teens) were demanded to gratify their sexual lusts. Throughout their twenty-year occupation, Timorese women have suffered constant sexual harassment from Indonesian garrison troops, harassment which flows from the very nature of the Indonesian occupation with its pervasive culture of violence and sustained abuse of human rights, as well as the deep psychological need experienced by an insecure occupation force to prove their 'potency' in the face of widespread local resistance and the fighting capacity of the male population.

Today, while individual acts of rape are more rare, there are still enormous pressures – physical and economic – on Timorese women to provide sexual services for Indonesian soldiers: some are forced into a position of 'kept women' for the armed men who are bivouacked in their villages, others, usually in those areas where the presence of the Falintil guerrillas is still strong – for example, in the east (Lautem/Lospalos) and central-eastern districts (Manatuto and Baucau) – are able to insist on soldiers going through a traditional dowry-payment ceremony (*barlaque*) and church marriage before being allowed to live with them. But even here, the relationship usually remains a distinctly unequal one, with Timorese 'wives' often being abandoned when soldiers return home to inner-island Indonesia.

Abuse of power by the Indonesian military took on other, more horrific, forms. As we have seen, torture was used from the very start, and the dreaded BAKIN (Indonesian State Intelligence Agency) interrogation rooms in the Hotel Tropical in Dili, and Hotel Flamboyan in Baucau, were always full. Starting with beatings, cigarette burnings, and sexual abuse, the torturers progressed rapidly to electric-shock treatment, systematic cutting of the skin with razor blades, the crushing of limbs (the favourite Indonesian method was to force a prisoner to place a hand or foot under a chair which was then sat upon by a heavy interrogator), water immersion and the extraction of finger- and toe-nails. Sometimes, these proceedings were watched by senior officers, such as Colonel Sinaga, a Sumatran who was later to become the principal Indonesian official (*Sekwilda*; Provincial Secretary) in the newly-constituted 'Provisional Government of East Timor' and right-hand man to the first Indonesian-appointed Governor of Timor, Arnaldo dos Reis Araújo (in office, July 1976–September 1978). Known as the 'Black God' to the Timorese, he was widely feared for his sadistic cruelty, and evident relish in forcing the confessions of

23

Timorese suspects. His record was matched by the appropriately named Batak Colonel (later General) Adolf Sahala Rajagukguk, who later drew up a manual detailing techniques for the extraction of information from prisoners and precautions needed when taking photographs of torture victims (July 1982). When, eventually, Suharto wished to reward this British Staff College-trained officer with the plum post of Ambassador to the United States in the early 1990s, even the normally understanding State Department appears to have had difficulty stomaching the idea of having a war criminal on the Washington diplomatic circuit (especially when new US laws made him liable for charges of crimes against humanity), so he was sent to New Delhi instead, a place more understanding of Asian 'values'.

Stalemate (January 1976–September 1977)

Despite the proud boast of General Murdani and his commanders that they 'would breakfast in Dili, lunch in Baucau and dine in Lospalos', thus wrapping up the East Timor campaign in a single day, it took the Indonesians until Christmas (ie nearly three weeks after the invasion) before they had full control of Dili. On 10 December, a second invasion force had been landed at Baucau to take the island's second town and principal airfield (capable of accommodating modern jet aircraft, and immediately used by the Indonesians for their airforce), and on 25–26 December substantial reinforcements (10–15,000 troops) were brought in to stiffen the attack, with further landings being made at Liquiçá and Maubara to the west of Dili, where most of the resident Chinese communities were killed. By April 1976, Indonesian forces in Timor had risen to 42,000 – over a quarter of the combat strength of their entire army – with 10,000 stationed in West Timor, and the rest deployed in operations in the east.

The day after the invasion (8 December), the Portuguese had abandoned Atauro and sailed for Darwin, thus bringing to an end over 460 years of involvement with Timor, which had begun with the Portuguese voyages of exploration in the early sixteenth century. It was an ignominious finale to a ruthless and remarkable chapter of Lusitanian history, one which had bequeathed a colonial culture more distinct and tenacious than any in the bloody annals of European expansion. In a different epoch, the crews of the newly commissioned Portuguese corvettes, *João Roby* and *Afonso Cerqueira* might have sailed forth under cover of darkness to do battle with the ageing Soviet-supplied warships of the Indonesian invasion force. But this was 1975, not 1514, nor even 1961, when the Salazarist navy had made a doomed attempt to protect Goa against the invading Indians. Instead, they slunk away across the Timor Sea, guns and torpedo tubes silent, never to appear again in Indonesian waters. These were not the men of whom Camões had written his epic *Os Lusíadas*, nor the descendants of the sixteenth-century warrior navigators.

On the diplomatic front, the Portuguese did request an urgent meeting of the UN Security Council to consider a motion calling for the immediate withdrawal of all Indonesian troops and a genuine act of self-determination, and this was duly passed on 23 December (a resolution repeated on 22 April 1976). At the same time, the Secretary-General was requested to send a fact-finding mission to East Timor to establish contact with all parties in the territory, a task entrusted to a special representative, Vittorio Winspeare Guiccardi, who visited Dili on 18 January, but was unable to visit Fretilin-held areas. Guiccardi's subsequent attempts to make contact with Fretilin via a local transmitter in Darwin were stymied by the Australian Government who promptly seized the 'unlicensed' radio equipment, and the Indonesians told him in no uncertain terms that his ship would be sunk should he attempt to reach Fretilin areas by sea (the Portuguese were contemplating putting one of their corvettes at his disposal). He thus returned to New York his mission aborted.

Guiccardi's useless peregrinations mirrored the almost total ineffectiveness of the UN with regard to the Timor issue, an ineffectiveness ensured by the reluctance of any of Indonesia's Western backers to bring meaningful pressure to bear on Jakarta. 'If it [comes] to the crunch and there [is] a row at the United Nations we should keep our heads down and avoid siding against the Indonesian Government', the British Ambassador in Jakarta had put it in a nutshell the previous July, and his sentiments were echoed by his colleague, US Ambassador David Newsom, who hoped that if Indonesia invaded Timor they would do so 'effectively, quickly, and not use our equipment'. In fact, US equipment (Hercules transport planes, M16 machine-guns, side arms etc) were used extensively in the invasion, and, despite a State Department charade, staged for the benefit of Congress, that the US Military Assistance Program was to be 'suspended' for six months, the flow of arms from existing contracts went on uninterrupted. Daniel Patrick Moynihan, the US Representative to the UN at this time, was later to boast in his memoirs that the US Administration had 'wished things to turn out as they did. . . . The Department of State desired that the UN prove utterly ineffective in whatever measures it undertook. The task was given to me, and I carried it forward with no inconsiderable success' (*A Dangerous Place* [Boston: Little, Brown and Company, 1978], p.247).

Vital though this diplomatic support and arms supplies were for the Indonesians, they could not overcome the gross incompetence of their military forces in the face of stiff Fretilin resistance. Pinned down on a narrow coastal strip around the capital, it took them over two years (January 1976–May 1978) before they could start moving against the principle Fretilin bases in the mountains, and towns such as Remexio and Railaco close to Dili changed hands many times before they were finally secured by the Indonesians in September 1978. The fact that many of the Indonesian troops were not paid for weeks on end, lacked adequate food supplies, and served under commanders who were prepared to make separate ceasefire arrangements with local Fretilin units – often to further their own trade deals with the resistance (high-quality Timorese coffee was bartered for rice [a lowland crop], sugar, imported medicines and other necessities, and the coffee was later sold on through Singapore by high-ranking officers involved with the East Timor campaign, who had set up their own trading company, PT Denok Hernandes International) – all militated against a zealous prosecution of the war.

During this time, in the zones under its control, where an estimated 500,000 Timorese civilians (two-thirds of the population) lived, Fretilin administration continued much as it had done during its three-month interregnum following the August–September 1975 civil war. Only now matters of military defense and the protection of the local communities against Indonesian attack were of crucial importance. At the Fretilin national conference at Soibada from 20 May to 2 June 1976, the decision was taken to fight a protracted 'people's war', any compromise with the Indonesians being ruled out. Falintil, originally established in August 1975, was now reshaped into a regular army, and small units, called 'shock brigades', were mustered to launch lightning attacks on Indonesian positions. Although arms were not in short supply following the capture of the Portuguese Taibesse arsenal, there was a problem of ammunition, so arrangements were made for the local manufacture of gunpowder in the Mount Matebian region using indigenous resources. Even at this early stage in the war, however, relations between the military and political wings of Fretilin were not straightforward. The influx of soldiers and NCOs from the Portuguese colonial army during the August–September 1975 civil war had certainly strengthened Fretilin, giving it a vital military capacity, but there was a fundamental clash of political culture between the Fretilin leadership, who insisted that 'politics were in command' (ie that the military should place the demands of the political struggle first), and the professional soldiers, imbued with the Portuguese principle of *apartidarismo*, which held that the army should keep out of politics and that key decisions in military affairs should be taken without reference to the politicians. As the tide of war began to turn against Fretilin in 1977–78 with the consequent pressure on supplies, so Falintil commanders showed themselves increasingly reluctant to arm the peasantry or fight a genuine people's war, still less heed the instructions of the Fretilin political commissars.

An elderly Portuguese priest, Father Leoneto do Rego, who had been forced at gunpoint by Falintil soldiers to accompany them to the mountains, later gave an interesting account of life in these Fretilin-controlled areas stating that the food situation was satisfactory (certainly better than that in the Indonesian-occupied areas) until mid-1977. Not originally a Fretilin supporter, he soon came to admire the skill with which they introduced new high-altitude crops (maize, manioc, potatoes), continued their schools (and built more new ones than the Portuguese had done in the previous five centuries), developed their adult literacy programmes, and established a health service using traditional medicines extracted from local plants. In Father do Rego's view, Fretilin 'were conscious of what they were fighting for – independence. If they hadn't cared, then everything would have been finished.'

The welfare of ordinary Timorese – referred to by the Fretilin as the *maubere* – from the Mambai word *Mau Bere*, 'my brother' – lay at the heart of the Party's struggle for an independent East Timor, a struggle which was aimed at emancipating the rural inhabitants of Timor from the thrall of servitude and debt-bondage to traditional chiefs (*liurai*), and from the tyranny of tribalism, superstition and illiteracy (hence the stress on adult education). Before 1974, the term *maubere* had been synonymous with everything that was contemptible (in the eyes of the town-dwelling Portuguese and *civilizados*) about the ignorant and impoverished Timorese highland peasantry. Now Fretilin was working to bring about a genuine social transformation – the transformation of the *maubere* into the true 'sons' and 'daughters' of Timor, citizens of an independent state.

The Portuguese priest's presence in the Fretilin zones – albeit initially forced – was indicative of a significant development in the Catholic Church in East Timor, one which would be of immense importance for the future. This was the change in the relationship between the Church and the people, and the growth of a ministry increasingly sensitive to the spiritual and national aspirations of ordinary Timorese. Throughout the colonial period, especially after the signature of the 1940 concordat between Rome and the Salazarist Government, the Catholic Church in East Timor had been an integral part of the colonial system. For much of this period, the Church was often the only symbol of Portuguese authority in rural areas, and it ran nearly all the colony's educational institutions (most of the Fretilin leaders, for example, were graduates of Catholic high schools, or the Catholic seminary at Daré, just outside Dili). Viewed as a foreign Church, it was alien to the majority of Timorese, who remained animists. Furthermore, the language used in the liturgy was

26

Portuguese or Latin – not Tetun – and, at times of political crisis, such as the Japanese occupation of 1941–45, the majority of Church personnel (very few of whom were Timorese) abandoned their parishes to seek refuge in Portugal or Australia.

All this changed with the Indonesian invasion: the priests and religious who remained were not able to leave, and many went with the local populations into the hills to escape the Indonesian army. Their links with Portugal severed and influenced by the rise of Timorese nationalism, they were forced to reconstruct their Church amid the carnage of war and foreign occupation. The Church's ministry thus became increasingly a people's ministry, one sensitive to the needs of Timorese Catholics rather than the Portuguese-speaking colonial elite, a change reflected in the decision of the Vatican to appoint a Timorese, Mgr. Martinho da Costa Lopes (in office, May 1977–May 1983), as Apostolic Administrator of the East Timor diocese when the Portuguese Bishop, Dom Joaquim Ribeiro, requested early retirement (he had been deeply traumatized by the killings in Dili) in 1977. Its decision to adopt Tetun in the liturgy rather than Indonesian, when Jakarta forbade the use of Portuguese in 1981, was also of immense significance, both for the development of the language, and for the growth of a Timorese national Church.

As in nineteenth-century Ireland, or Communist-ruled Poland, the Catholic Church in Timor became increasingly important as a vehicle for the expression of a specific national identity. Indeed, once Rome had taken over the direct administration of the East Timor diocese following the Indonesian invasion – rather than joining it with the Indonesian Bishops' Conference as the Indonesians wished – it was the *only* local institution capable of communicating independently with the outside world and of articulating the deep trauma of the Timorese people. The Church thus represented for the Timorese a precious continuity with the pre-invasion past, and a public space not filled by an alien occupying power. Although this development was still some way in the future during Father do Rego's enforced sojourn in the Fretilin zones in 1976–78, the remarkable growth of the Timorese Catholic community – by 1990 there would be nearly 680,000 registered communicants out of a total population of just under 750,000 – was already apparent.

The steady movement of the Timorese population away from the Indonesian-occupied towns and villages has often been portrayed by Jakarta as the result of Fretilin 'terror'. According to the Indonesians, Fretilin 'forced' the population to go with them into the hills. Apart from isolated individuals – Father do Rego is a case in point – there is no evidence to suggest this was the case. True, Fretilin was not guiltless of wanton acts of violence – the murder of 150 UDT and Apodeti prisoners (including the pro-integrationist party leader, José Osório Soares) whom Fretilin had taken to the mountains with them after the invasion, was one such tragic example. But, compared to the bloody excesses of the Indonesian invaders, it was a rare atrocity. The simple fact of the matter is that the Timorese fled because the Indonesians – in contravention of every rule of war and the dictates of common humanity – turned their guns on them. Today, East Timor is a land of crosses, mute testimony to the tens of thousands of ordinary civilians who were cut down in cold blood by the Indonesians. Cemeteries are full of mass graves – multiple white tombstones and black painted crosses with the names of the victims and dates of death simply incised – sometimes whole families killed on the same day. Countless unmarked sites of death also scar the island, the scattered bones of what were once living communities have now become the unhonoured dust of Timor's genocide. Not for them the carefully gathered ossuaries of contemporary Cambodia. For the Indonesians even commemorations are a threat.

After the atrocities committed in Dili, Maubara and Liquiçá in the early days of the war, the entire populations of neighbouring towns and villages abandoned their homes and sought refuge behind Fretilin lines. Of the 32,000 inhabitants of a district in Baucau who had 'presented themselves' as ordered to the Indonesian forces between the 10 December 1975 and the end of February 1976, fewer than 10,000 remained by the end of the year – the rest had fled to the mountains. This kind of flight was not undertaken lightly – it meant abandoning houses and fields often owned and cultivated for generations for the uncertainties of life in the highlands (Fretilin leaders had become increasingly concerned at their ability to meet the basic needs of so many civilians and even encouraged some to return to Indonesian-occupied areas as the war intensified in late 1977). But the ruthlessness of the Indonesians gave them no other choice.

It was at this time that the phenomenon of the 'dead earth' regions came into being. These were areas, hitherto inhabited and cultivated before the Indonesian invasion, from where the populations had fled in the 1975–77 period to escape the savagery of the occupiers. When Indonesian troops eventually moved into these regions, they set fire to the abandoned houses and drove off the remaining livestock. An empty house was a sure sign, in the the eyes of the Indonesians, that the previous inhabitants had gone to the mountains 'to join Fretilin', hence it was appropriate to destroy the property, partly as an act of revenge, partly to create a free-fire zone where Fretilin 'insurgents' could be hunted down at will. Many beautiful Timorese stilted houses with the traditional high-hipped thatched roofs and intricate carved woodwork were destroyed in this fashion never to be rebuilt: when the survivors came down from the hills after the terrible 'encirclement and annihilation' campaigns of 1978–79, they were not allowed to return to their original homes, but were forced into newly-built resettlement centres, mostly in insalubrious areas close to the main roads, where they eked out a miserable existence in galvanized-iron-roofed shacks.

Travelling across the wide plain from Fuiloro to Lospalos in the extreme east of the island in 1992, the travel writer Norman Lewis has left a vivid description of one such 'dead earth' region where sporadic fighting between the Falintil guerrillas and the Indonesian army is still taking place:

Down by the sea there had been villages, and faint rectangles drawn on the charcoal marked where the houses had stood. [. . .] Regular cultivation of the soil had come to an end with benefit to spontaneous and unaided growth. [. . .] The dead earth was marked out with what might have been taken for the inscriptions or traceries of pre-historic man, or even space-invaders. Rice paddies had been cut out here, tended, irrigated and fertilised for generations, and now what remained were meticulous geometrical shapes growing wildflowers to rejoice the heart of someone indifferent to husbandry. Flowers had sprung up everywhere in the vacated land: bright doodlings where ploughs had meandered through the rocks. . . . (*An Empire of the East: Travels in Indonesia* [London: Jonathan Cape, 1993], p.122)

Encirclement and annihilation
(September 1977–March 1979)

In September 1977, the Indonesian army launched a new campaign designed to undermine Fretilin resistance by destroying its base areas, especially its food production capacity.

The nearly two years of stalemate which had followed the December 1975 Indonesian invasion had proved increasingly embarrassing to Jakarta, exposing as it did the corruption and ineptitude of its armed forces, and the ineffectiveness of its civil administration in what the Indonesians now pretended was their '27th Province' (the bill integrating East Timor into the Indonesian Republic had been rushed through the rubber-stamp Indonesian Parliament on 17 July 1976 following the 'petition' to Suharto from the hastily assembled 28-member 'People's Representative Council of the Region of East Timor' meeting in the former Dili Sports Hall at the end of May). Criticism of Indonesia's actions had been growing in Western Europe, Australia and the United States, fanned by reports of Indonesian atrocities which reached the West from Catholic Church sources and the Fretilin radio link with Australia's Northern Territory. The unanimous condemnation of Indonesia at the Conference of Non-Aligned Movement (NAM) countries in Colombo in August 1976 had been galling also since Jakarta saw itself as one of the founders of this Movement (which dated back to the 1955 Asia-Africa Conference in Bandung) and coveted its chairmanship (which it eventually got in 1991, by which time the end of the Cold War had deprived the Movement of all meaning).

For the new campaign to be a success, Jakarta had first to obtain new weapons for its armed forces. Money was not a problem (the oil price bonanza of December 1973 had quadrupled Indonesia's government revenues almost overnight), but unless sophisticated weapons systems – particularly counter-insurgency aircraft – were made available from the West, the military stalemate in East Timor looked set to continue. It is here that Western responsibility for the Timor tragedy becomes most evident: the willingness of Western governments to sell Indonesia the required equipment not only sealed the fate of the pre-1979 Timorese resistance, but also ensured that this victory would be bought at the cost of maximum civilian casualties.

The United States was pivotal, for it was, at this time, Indonesia's principal arms supplier and provider of military training. The rhetoric of the new US President, Jimmy Carter (1977–81), with his 'human rights' agenda, had alarmed Suharto. What if this extended to Indonesia and East Timor? His concern was unjustified. Less than a month after Carter had taken office (January 1977), 13 OV-10F 'Bronco' counter-insurgency aircraft manufactured by the Rockwell International Corporation had been delivered to Indonesia courtesy of an official US Government foreign military sales credit. Known to the Timorese as 'scorpions' because of their black fuselage and curved-back tail wing, these were ideally suited for use in East Timor. As a low-flying, relatively slow-moving aircraft, they were capable of pinpointing resistance positions in difficult terrain and under varying climactic conditions. The fact that their payload could include napalm, chemical and biological weapons, and high-explosive (1000 pound) bombs capable of blowing craters in rock, was apparently of no concern to their American suppliers.

These aircraft – soon joined by 16 A-4E Skyhawk bombers (built by the American McDonnell-Douglas company) – were immediately in action in the skies over East Timor. Flying from the newly converted airbase at Baucau, they made daily sorties over the Fretilin-held areas in the mountains, while naval guns pounded villages nearer the coast. With the Indonesian army in Timor now reinforced by fifteen new battalions (12,000 men), 'search-and-destroy' operations were pushed into the interior, systematically wiping out populations suspected of Fretilin sympathies. A Dili-based priest spoke of 'hundreds' of deaths every day, with bodies being left where they fell on the bare mountainsides to become food for carnivorous birds. The use of chemical and biological weapons (Agent Orange defoliant, for example) and napalm was widely confirmed: survivors spoke of children dying of violent attacks of vomiting and dysentery after drinking water in bombed areas, of crop-destroying maggots (*ular kecil*) emerging within a few days of bombing raids, and of whole communities incinerated alive when tinder-dry *palapa* (palm thatch) houses went up in flames. So intense were the bombardments in some places, and so toxic the substances used, that local people described how they saw rocks turn white, and trees and scrub disintegrate under the 'rain' spewed from the aircraft.

Those who tried to surrender to the Indonesians found little mercy: women and young girls were physically abused and raped (some of those already pregnant had their abdomens ripped open), and their menfolk killed when they tried to protect them. Many civilians fled back into the bush, preferring to die fighting in Fretilin-held areas, rather than be humiliated and gunned down like wild animals. The fate of Fretilin soldiers and their families, especially those in senior positions or 'intellectuals' with political influence (long hair was often taken as a sign of this status), was worse: some were killed by being hurled from helicopters over the open sea, others were tortured to death. Chilling euphemisms now began to enter the vocabulary of the Indonesian intelligence officers reflecting favoured methods of execution – *'mandi di laut'* ('[going] for a bathe in the sea'), *'menghinap di Hotel Flamboyan'* ('staying the night in the Hotel Flamboyan [in Baucau]'), *'piknik ke Builico'* ('going on a picnic to Builico [Ainaro]', a place where prisoners were killed by being hurled off the Hatu Builico cliffs), and *'berjalan ke Quelicai'* ('taking a trip to Quelicai', the notorious Quelicai river bank in the central-eastern sector where hundreds of Fretilin supporters died, a site the local inhabitants came to call the 'second hell' [*segundo inferno*]).

Sometimes executions took place in public as a form of barbaric spectacle. One such was witnessed by a Timorese schoolteacher in Baucau, who told how the victims were suspended by their feet from a high wall in one of the main thoroughfares of the town in full view of a group of watching children. They were then stoned and bludgeoned to death with the butts of rifles, the Indonesians cutting down the corners of their mouths with their stabbing knives in mock clown smiles and slicing off their genitals. A day later the head of another Timorese captured on Mount Matebian was paraded around the streets on a pole followed by a crowd of boys and girls. 'As a teacher it sickens me that children see such things', this witness admitted, '[But] you couldn't call [them] away; no, that would be too dangerous; for the Indonesians that would mean you are opposing them.' (Michele Turner, *Telling. East Timor: Personal Testimonies, 1942–92* [Kensington: New South Wales University Press, 1992], pp.176–77).

For those Fretilin suspects whose lives were initially spared, the Indonesians had prepared a form of living death on the island of Atauro, refuge of the last Portuguese Governor, now a vast prison camp. Many of the 5000 detained here in 1982, the Gulag's peak year, were families of still active members of the resistance. Packed into little plastic-sheeted shacks under the relentless sun of this virtually treeless volcanic island, their rations consisted of 900 grams of maize a month and they were forced to sell everything they had just to support themselves. Within the space of just two-and-a-half years nearly 400 died of gastro-enteritis and intestinal disorders, young children and elderly people being especially at risk. Although the prison island was eventually closed in the late 1980s, most of its inmates were transferred to other detention centres and concentration camps in

East Timor itself, places such as Cailaco (near the West Timor border), Comarca (the century-old colonial prison in Dili) and Baucau, where detainees continued to die of starvation, disease and neglect. 'When they took me to Atauro,' one previous inmate confided, 'they put me in a coffin for four months. It's dark. You hear nothing, you see nothing and it just fits your body. When you come out all you want to do is run about. Sometimes they made you drag an iron bar to quieten you down [. . . .] Four years on Atauro, another four in Cai-Laco. It leaves its mark. You're never the same again.' (Lewis, *Empire of the East*, p.136).

One particularly sinister Indonesian tactic was the recruitment of Timorese to fight against their fellow countrymen: two Timorese battalions (744 and 745) had been set up in 1976, and many Timorese were conscripted into the local civil defense (*Hansip –Pertahanan Sipil*) units. Apart from a few Apodeti volunteers, most had little enthusiasm for such military activities, especially when they found that they were forced to march in front of the main Indonesian formations during the encirclement campaign, and were treated as inferior beings by their Javanese officers (the racism of inner-island Indonesians was constantly resented, especially as it stood in such marked contrast to the lack of racial prejudice of the former Portuguese authorities and the relaxed *mestiço* [mixed race] culture of the colonial era).

Given this resentment, it is hardly surprising that the Timorese *Hansip* units, in particular, proved unreliable for the Indonesians. Among the many incidents of mutiny was one which was to have dire consequences for the local population. This occurred some years after the 1977–78 'encirclement and annihilation' operation and came during an unofficial ceasefire between Fretilin and the Indonesian forces (March–August 1983), when the latter had undoubtedly dropped their guard. A *Hansip* unit in the small village of Kraras near Viqueque close to the south coast, turned on a contingent of seventeen Indonesian soldiers (army engineers), killing them with knives, clubs and other implements while they were resting at night. They then seized their weapons and fled into the bush to join up with Fretilin. This incident on 8 August 1983, which marked the end of the ceasefire, provoked the Indonesians into an act of terrible revenge: nearly all the village's inhabitants – between 200 to 300 people – were murdered, many being forced over a steep cliff-face, others being burnt alive in their houses. To this day this village – Timor's Oradour-sur-Glâne – has not been rebuilt and the Indonesians have not permitted crosses to be placed on the mass graves.

As the Indonesian noose tightened around Fretilin at the end of 1977, and more and more food-producing areas came under attack from the air, so tensions in the resistance leadership mounted. Xavier do Amaral, the 40-year old Jesuit-educated Fretilin President, who had argued for compromise with the Indonesians in order to save civilian lives, attempted a coup and was arrested (7 September). His place was taken by Nicolau Lobato, whose qualities of leadership and military prowess had already been amply demonstrated in the fighting against the Indonesians since 1975. A year later (30 August 1978), abandoned by his guards, Amaral was captured by the Indonesians in the central highlands and later ended up in Bali in the house of the first Indonesian army commander in East Timor, General Dading Kalbuadi, where he lived as a sort of house boy.

In May 1978, after a lull in the fighting, the Indonesians launched a new operation. Codenamed 'Skylight', this was designed to break the Fretilin leadership by provoking defections to the Indonesian side. Alarico Fernandes, the Fretilin Minister of Information, who was responsible for maintaining radio links with the outside world (via transmitters in Australia's Northern Territory) and who may have ordered the execution of some of the UDT/Apodeti prisoners in December 1975, was persuaded to co-operate. Like Amaral, he had begun to doubt the efficacy of the Fretilin policy of self-reliance in the face of overwhelming Indonesian military power, especially in the light of the lack of hoped for support from socialist countries. He succeeded in persuading several Falintil commanders and regional political commissars of the futility of continuing the war, and sent secret radio messages to Indonesian intelligence revealing the location of some resistance units. As a result, when Fernandes and his family gave themselves up to the Indonesians in September 1978, he brought with him many other important Falintil fighters, who believed that their surrender would hasten a political solution to the war. All were executed by the Indonesians, and Fernandes himself was eventually exiled to the remote eastern Indonesian island of Sumba after being forced to watch his wife and daughter being raped in front of him by his Indonesian guards.

Fernandes's defection marked the beginning of the end for organized Fretilin resistance in the two remaining redoubt areas of Mount Matebian in the east and the Natarbora plain near the south coast. Rising to over 9000 feet, its sides clad in dense forests riven with limestone clefts and gorges, Matebian – 'Soul Mountain' in Tetun – has a particular place in Timorese folklore. Revered as the abode of the departed souls of the Timorese (Belu) ancestors, it has been a place of sanctuary since pre-history. In times of trouble, villagers from a wide area would take refuge there in the belief that the thick sandalwood stands would make them invisible to their pursuers, while the abundance of grubs, insects, edible roots and leaves would assure them of food. It was here, in the closing months of 1978, that the final act of Fretilin's first period of resistance to the Indonesians was played out.

By 17 October, Indonesian troops were at the foot of the mountain where 160,000 Timorese fighters and civilians were now holding out. Struggling through the dense undergrowth of Matebian's foothills, they tried to advance, but were cut down by the Falintil units, suffering upwards of 3,000 casualties within the first two months (October and November). It was then that the Indonesians started saturation bombing. Morning and afternoon, their planes flew overhead – Broncos and Skyhawks taking it in turns to drop their deadly payloads. During the day, the population hid in caves, emerging only at night. Some were entombed alive when high-explosive bombs blasted their rock shelters, others were caught in the open by napalm. By 4 December, the Fretilin units had lost radio contact and food supplies were at an end. The leadership announced that they could no longer protect the people and urged surrender. Hearing this, many wept. Everyone had to decide for themselves whether to stay or go. By now Falintil had begun to split up to fight on as separate guerrilla units, and civilians had to make shift as best they could in the face of the Indonesian onslaught. The hillside was littered with unburied bodies. Nearly all the forest animals had fled. Soul Mountain was giving up its secrets.

While this tragedy was unfolding, the Fretilin leader Nicolau Lobato was being pursued relentlessly by Indonesian helicopter-borne special forces. Eventually, on 31 December, he was cornered on Mount Maubisse in the hills 50 kilometres south of Dili. After a six-hour gun-battle, commenced just before dawn, he was captured by units of Timorese Battalion 744 led by Lieutenant (now Brigadier-General) Yunus Yosfiah, and troops under the command of Suharto's future son-in-law, Lieutenant (now Colonel) Prabowo Subianto

Djojohadikusumo. Mortally wounded in the stomach, the 32-year-old Fretilin President died in the helicopter taking him to Dili, where his mutilated corpse was displayed to the exultant Indonesian Defense Minister, Andi Muhammad Yusuf, who had flown to East Timor for the victory celebrations, the whole incident of Lobato's capture and death being recorded on video for the benefit of the Indonesian military (Yosfiah's favourite pastime now being to watch endless re-runs of his star role in this film). It seemed as though the war in East Timor had been won.

Famine, resettlement and the rebirth of the Timorese Resistance (1979–88)

'If Indonesia thinks that by exterminating Falintil the war will end, they are wrong!' These words, spoken by José Alexandre (Xanana) Gusmão, Lobato's successor as the leader of the Timorese national resistance, to the Australian lawyer, Robert Domm, in September 1990, encapsulated Indonesia's problem. They might have destroyed Falintil's capacity to fight as a conventional army, but they had not blunted the Timorese will to survive as an independent nation. *'Pátria ou Morte!'* ('Fatherland or Death!') remained the cry in every heart. The more terrible the repression, the more determined the Timorese were to win through.

Seen from the dark days of January 1979, that determination might have seemed futile. After all, the Indonesians were mopping up the remaining resistance in the Matebian redoubt, and the surviving civilian populations in the highland areas (between 250,000 and 350,000) were being herded down into resettlement camps where many were to die of starvation in the ensuing months – the scorched earth tactics of the Indonesians and displacement of highland communities having had a devastating effect on local food supplies. A whole way of life – that of the shifting 'slash-and-burn' (swidden) cultivators of the mountain regions with their small scattered hamlets (*povoacão*) – was now being destroyed in the interests of the Indonesian tactic of 'separating the people from the terrorists'.

Although the Indonesian authorities pretended that the resettlement camps were a means of bringing welfare services 'closer to the people', their underlying logic was overwhelmingly military. Like the 'strategic hamlets' of Vietnam War vintage, they were part and parcel of an ongoing counter-insurgency campaign aimed at denying Falintil the support of the local people. Like the Americans, however, the Indonesians soon found that their effect against a well-organized and strongly supported local nationalist movement was very limited. Many civilians were to die before this lesson was learnt.

The number of civilian deaths during the 1979 famine will never be known exactly. Some estimates indicate that the death rate in the resettlement camps was in the region of 2500 a month (ie 1 per cent of the total camp population) throughout most of 1979, a situation exacerbated by the delays imposed by the Indonesian authorities in allowing vital food assistance to reach East Timor from the West: it was only in August that the first relief shipments began to arrive and by then it was too late for many (even so the Indonesian army still sought to make a profit out of the tragedy by hiring out their helicopters at US$850 an hour to the relief agencies). Western observers spoke of conditions as bad as Biafra and Cambodia.

The situation in the resettlement camps was made worse by the fact the Indonesians refused to allow the inhabitants to go further than a few hundred meters from the camp perimeters to cultivate fields for fear that they would make contact with the resistance. This, combined with the fact that many of the camps were in insalubrious, malaria-ridden areas, where the soil was eroded or acidic, greatly reduced the amount of food which could be produced. Another problem was that of water, with many wells having been poisoned or destroyed by the Indonesians during the war, and other sources, such as mountain springs and streams, being 'out of bounds' to the civilian populations in the camps. The shortage of water and the means to extract it forced whole communities to dig for it wherever possible.

The famine, which continued in some places right through into the 1981–82 planting season, when the drafting of the population into the infamous 'fence of legs' (*Operasi Kikis*) operation to flush out remaining Fretilin fighters in rural areas again put pressure on food supplies, was thus a direct result of Indonesian wartime tactics and subsequent resettlement policy. So much livestock (particularly buffalo and cattle) had been killed during the 'encirclement and annihilation' campaign, that fields could not be prepared for planting nor organic fertilizer obtained. The Indonesian Government later compounded this problem by awarding thousands of hectares of 'underutilized' ricefields, especially in the Maliana plain area close to the Indonesian border, to Balinese and Javanese 'transmigrants', without any compensation to the original owners (who were now either dead or languishing in resettlement camps). They argued that the East Timorese 'needed to be taught better farming techniques', as if there had been no previous history of Timorese rice cultivation before the Indonesian invasion. Thus old-fashioned colonialism and plunder began to masquerade in the guise of 'development'.

Now that the Indonesians could at last claim to control the territory of East Timor (apart from those areas in the east where clashes with Fretilin guerrillas were still taking place), they began to conduct a detailed census of the population. Their first, in June 1979, purported to show that there were just over half a million people (516,517) living in the province, a figure which had supposedly risen to 567,000 in 1981. It is not known whether these figures also included the large number of Indonesian civilians in the territory, but it is significant that the statistics produced by the Timorese Catholic Church at this time (1981) show a very much smaller surviving Timorese population of some 425,000. Prior to the Indonesian invasion, there had been just under 700,000 people living in Timor, and the population was growing at around 2.2 per cent a year. Even if we assume that this rate of natural growth was halved due to the intensity of the conflict and the subsequent famine, there should still have been around 732,000 people in the province by 1981. Where had the missing 308,000 (170,000, if we believe the Indonesian statistics) got to? Since only a modest number of Timorese refugees (perhaps 6000) had made it to the West (Australia and Portugal) by this time, the only conclusion is that they were dead. This means that, since their December 1975 invasion, the Indonesians have been directly responsible for the deaths of between a quarter and a third of the local population, one of the worst levels of mortality of any society since the Second World War – even in Pol Pot's Cambodia (1975–78) civilian deaths did not exceed a fifth of the pre-1975 citizenry.

As the years have passed, so senior Indonesian officials have begun to admit to the scale of the demographic disaster which overwhelmed Timor after 1975. Already, in April 1977, former Foreign Minister Adam Malik in an interview with a leading Australian newspaper observed that, in the first sixteen months of fighting (December 1975–March 1977), 'perhaps 80,000 might have been killed [. . .] in East Timor [. . . .] It was war [. . . .] Then what is all the big fuss?'. Two years later, his successor, Dr Mochtar Kusumaatmadja, admitted in a press briefing in London that 120,000 had died in East Timor since the start of the 'civil war' in 1975. More recently (April 1994), the new Indonesian-appointed Governor of East Timor, Abílio Soares (in office, September 1992–present), in an interview with the London *Economist*, remarked that a figure of between 100,000 and 200,000 for the number of deaths sustained in East Timor as a direct result of the fighting after 1975 'was probably correct'. The fiction that all these casualties were due to Fretilin 'terror' and the ongoing 'fratricidal civil war' between the Timorese parties after August 1975 had now begun to wear thin.

While the Indonesians were assessing the demographic consequences of their East Timor conquest, and the surviving Timorese population were struggling for survival in the resettlement camps, the Fretilin leadership was coming to terms with the crippling losses it had sustained during the 1977–79 period. At its National Conference at Mabai (Lacluta) in March 1981, the first after the fall of Mount Matebian, they noted the following: 85 per cent of the members of the Supreme Command killed (only two [Ma'Huno, Xanana Gusmão] of the Fretilin Central Committee who remained in East Timor after 7 December 1975 had survived and these were both subsequently captured by the Indonesians); 80 per cent of Falintil troops lost, together with 90 per cent of their weapons; all Fretilin support bases destroyed and Indonesian troops in control of the surviving population; all lines of communication between the remaining resistance fighters – outside the eastern zone (Lospalos, Ponta Leste) – severed, and communications with the outside world cut (there had been no contact with the Fretilin mission abroad, led by José Ramos-Horta, since Alarico Fernandes's defection in September 1978), making it impossible to channel information to supporters overseas.

The first task of the Fretilin leadership was to restore links between the scattered Falintil units still capable of mounting attacks on Indonesian positions. Once these had been established, pre-1979 military and political strategies were completely revised: the policy of maintaining fixed bases was abandoned – Falintil units were now to function as highly mobile columns, continually moving from place to place. At the same time, a network of clandestine organizations was set up behind enemy lines in the resettlement camps and population centres under Indonesian control. The vital links between the armed resistance movement in the bush and the clandestine organizations in the camps and towns was henceforth maintained through the *nurep* ('*núcleos de resistência popular*' or 'popular resistance centres') which had a presence in most inhabited areas.

Reliance of weaponry strength, the hallmark of the old-style Falintil, was now replaced by reliance on the strength of the people with guerrilla units henceforth being made responsible for securing their own food supplies (from abandoned village gardens and fields), weapons and ammunition (from captured Indonesian equipment). Through the *nurep*, the Fretilin guerrillas were able to obtain key equipment such as radios, tape-recorders and batteries, which enabled them to keep in touch with one another and with the outside world.

The new strategy adopted at the 1981 Conference, was remarkably successful. By March 1983, on the initiative of local Indonesian commanders a whole series of local ceasefires had been arranged, which later resulted in a general ceasefire (23 March–

8 August 1983) and the opening of negotiations between Xanana and Colonel Purwanto, the commander of the East Timor 'Security Operations Command' (*Komando Operasi Keamanan* / KOOPSKAM). The fact that Fretilin had been able to make such a comeback from near total defeat within the space of three short years was a measure both of Xanana's exceptional political skills, and the continued support of the local Timorese population for the resistance cause.

A native of Manatuto in the central-eastern area of Timor, Xanana (born 1946) had been a construction worker under the Portuguese. As a militant member of ASDT/Fretilin, he had been elected a member of the Fretilin Central Committee serving in the Department of Information during the *de facto* Fretilin administration in the last quarter of 1975. After the Indonesian invasion, he had become Deputy-Secretary of the regional command of the central-eastern sector and was put in charge of a Falintil platoon, before moving to the Ponta Leste (extreme eastern) region as sector commander at the time of the 1977–78 Indonesian offensive. After the fall of Mount Matebian and the collapse of organized Fretilin resistance, he took provisional control of Falintil as Commander-in-Chief, during which time he wrote (in Portuguese) two theoretical works – *Country and Revolution* and *Themes on the War*, which describe the revolutionary process of a people's war based on his experiences of the struggle in East Timor. The architect of the post-1979 reorganization of Fretilin and Falintil, he is now the undisputed leader of the Timorese resistance within Timor itself – and continues to be so regarded despite his capture in November 1992 and imprisonment by the Indonesians (he is currently serving a 20-year sentence in Jakarta's Cipinang jail). A man cut in the mould of Nelson Mandela, he is destined to become the first President of an independent East Timor.

In the aftermath of the 1978–79 disaster, Xanana showed a remarkable capacity to rethink the whole direction of the resistance struggle. After his success in rebuilding Falintil after 1979 and reorientating it towards a mobile guerrilla war, he realized that it was no longer enough to see the struggle as synonymous with Fretilin. Much debate had taken place between the surviving Fretilin and Falintil leaders concerning the causes and consequences of the military collapse, and the idea of forming a new 'Revolutionary Council of National Resistance' (*Conselho Revolucionária de Resistência Nacional* or CRRN), as the supreme body of the resistance, had already been mooted at a meeting of commanders in March 1979. It officially came into being at the historic conference at Mabai (Lacluta) in March 1981, when Xanana was chosen as its leader. He was determined that this new organization would serve as an umbrella for all the various nationalist groups fighting for Timorese independence, both inside and outside Timor. He knew that if it was seen as a purely Fretilin front, the others would not join. So he announced at the second Fretilin national conference in 1984, that although he would remain Commander-in-Chief of Falintil, he would no longer remain a member of Fretilin (he even returned his party card), but would henceforth stand above party politics. Already, under his political direction, Fretilin had dropped its leftist stance and publicly accepted the need for a multi-party system. Now he made overtures to Fretilin's erstwhile coalition partner, the right of centre UDT. These were successful, and in March 1986 the Fretilin external delegation in Lisbon announced the formation of a new nationalist 'convergence' between the two parties, with the CRRN becoming the 'National Council for Maubere Resistance' (*Conselho Nacional de Resistência Maubere* or CNRM) under Xanana's presidency. At the same time, Falintil, the former Fretilin army, was transformed into the national army of East Timor. With the adherence of East Timorese Students' National Resistance (*Resistência Nacional Estudantil de Timor Leste* or Renetil) movement, a genuine national front had come into being which embraced all political parties and groups dedicated to securing national independence.

Xanana's diplomatic skills were again on display when he met with the Indonesian commander, Colonel Purwanto, at Lariguto (Ossu) on 21–23 March 1983 to arrange the general ceasefire, which was later annulled by General Murdani, and in the mid- to late 1980s when he negotiated with the new Apostolic Administrator (post-1988, Bishop) of Dili, Mgr. Carlos Filipe Ximenes Belo (in office, May 1983 to present) to obtain the support of the Church for the independence struggle. Given the resistance leader's political stature, it is inevitable that the Indonesian government will have to open talks with him if they are serious about reaching a solution to the East Timor problem.

What sort of a man is Xanana? Robert Domm, the Australian lawyer who made a hazardous journey to his mountain camp in September 1990, was struck first by his rather tall distinguished-looking appearance with his healthy growth of beard and ready smile:

Xanana was fine, a person with the capacity to relax. He had a good sense of humour, obviously a very careful and intelligent person, but he could switch off and it was easy, almost like talking to [a friend]. When he switched on again, there was the military commander, but a friendly likeable sort of bloke.

Beneath the charm there was the steely toughness of the classic guerrilla leader, the combination of clear-headed intellect and soldierly discipline. 'Meeting him', Domm continued, 'I could understand the reverence in which ordinary Timorese hold him. He's a living symbol of their resistance.'

In conversation, Xanana showed a remarkable grasp of the political dimensions of the struggle, both within Timor itself and more widely. He had immediately understood, for example, the significance for Timor of the Western response to Saddam Hussein's August 1990 invasion of Kuwait and the issue of protecting small states against predatory neighbours. In terms of the military contest, the Timorese leader was realistic:

In the current situation, the guerrillas try to minimize their great difficulties. After [so many] years, obviously everyone understands that without any support from outside, Falintil can't think about great military successes. The enemy's current tactic is to suffocate us with constant military action, and we try to neutralize and accommodate each attack.

He talked frankly of the pressures caused by the increasingly sophisticated Indonesian counter-insurgency tactics: during the 1981 'fence of legs' (*pagar betis*) campaign, the notorious Operasi Kikis operation, almost the entire Timorese population were treated as inferior beings and used as 'beaters' walking in great lines through the bush, with Indonesian soldiers at their backs, in an attempt to flush out the guerrillas; the 1983–84 campaign involving almost the entire Indonesian arsenal – warships, tanks, bombers, mortars, cannons – 'in battalions we got tired of counting'; the shift of tactic in 1986–87 to the use of elite troops (*Kopassus*) in what Xanana termed 'territorial guerrilla warfare', warfare which involved relatively small numbers of military personnel operating according to a well-defined plan, with short bursts of activity in which Indonesian forces would fan out in small groups; the new large-scale offensive in 1988, and, finally, the increased use of Timorese conscripts in highly mobile counter-insurgency warfare. 'This makes it very difficult for us to take initiatives', Xanana admitted, 'because we don't have a permanent, fixed enemy. [They have] no real volume or quantity; and we don't know what to confront. We feel that the enemy is everywhere; we even say that we carry them in our bags!'

What sort of guerrilla force could possibly survive under such conditions? Xanana spoke of their mobility 'in the whole sense of that word. Without even the minimum capacity to supply ourselves with weapons and ammunition, without the capacity to create production zones to supply ourselves, without the minimum conditions to [cultivate] some piece of land, a small factory to make our own clothing, you can understand our difficulties.' These difficulties were overcome by the almost preternatural way the guerrillas went about their business. Domm noticed:

They wore military boots, but they moved like cats. Everything they did was done silently and gently. When they smoked their hand would be cupped around so as not to show the light; they listened to the short-wave radio on the lowest possible volume, they cooked on coals without smoke. [. . . .] They were constantly aware of each other, working together without the need for much speech. [. . . .] When we were in thick bush the atmosphere wasn't tense any more: this was their territory. They said five of them could pin down an Indonesian force of up to a hundred while we escaped. They had a strong rapport with each other, with the local people, and the scouts we met along the way. I felt safe with them. They blended into the bush; it was the Indonesians who were at a disadvantage here, it must have been real ambush country for them.

'It's our political motivation that sustains us in this war.' Xanana explained, 'It's too great for us to lose, our morale is unshakeable and this allows us to overcome all our difficulties. In such a small territory, surrounded by sea on all sides and with a naval blockade imposed by the enemy, you can understand our difficulties.' Despite the enormous risks, however, there was always a large reserve of young men waiting to go to the mountains if called on. Numbers of fighters (currently between 500 and 1000) were restricted not by want of recruits, but by the limits of the resources available. [All quotes from Official Transcript Background Briefing, 28, 29, 30 October 1990, broadcast on ABC Radio National. Report from The Mountains of East Timor: Interview with Resistance Guerilla Commander, Shanana (sic) Gusmão.]

Even for the network of Timorese civilians who sustained them in their day-to-day operations, there were constant dangers. Anyone, young or old, suspected of having contacts with the resistance or denounced by the ubiquitous spy (bufo) network, was subjected to beatings and torture. Indeed, Indonesian soldiers and police were rewarded when a person confessed to such links. For ordinary Timorese the cost was very high. Today, black-hooded death squads linked to the military, known as ninja, terrorize the local population, kidnapping suspects and torturing them to death. Every family can recount a tale of personal tragedy, of the knock on the door at night, of relatives who have 'disappeared' after being taken in for questioning. A multitude of fears engulfs everyday life.

Yet, despite all these pressures, the resistance continues. The guerrillas still control most of the mountainous spine of the country, the great 10,000-foot peaks like Mount Ramelau and Mount Tatamailau ('The grandparents in the heights' in Tetun) from where they fight in small groups of three or four, liaising with their home villages and mounting ambushes against the Indonesians. These mountains are not just useful military vantage points: in the traditional animist culture of the Timorese, they are sacred places. 'The presence of the guerrillas has a deep political meaning', according to Xanana's successor as operational commander, ex-primary school teacher Konis Santana. 'When our people look up at the mountains, they know it is where their children are, where their arms are raised in rebellion.'

The willingness of so many young Timorese to come up into the mountains to take the place of fallen comrades is testimony to the failure of the Indonesians to win over the successor generation in Timor to the idea of 'integration'. Indeed, the very word 'integrasi' has become synonymous for most Timorese with Indonesian colonialism and its persecution of Timorese culture and society.

After the genocide of the late 1970s came the 'ethnocide' of the 1980s, when Timor was subjected to a more subtle death, not physical this time (although arbitrary executions and massacres continued), but spiritual, the destruction of Timor's specific cultural heritage derived from its pre-colonial past and its four-and-a-half centuries of Portuguese contact. It was this loss which Bishop Belo was later to refer to in his letter of 6 February 1989 to the UN Secretary-General calling for a UN-supervised referendum in the territory and warning that the Timorese were 'dying as a people and as a nation'.

The insistence on the use of Indonesian (*Bahasa*) in schools, the influx of mainly Muslim settlers and officials from inner-island Indonesia (by the early 1990s nearly all primary school teachers in the country were Muslim), the insensitivity of the occupation forces to Timorese Catholicism (even to the point of the desecration of the host), the clumsy attempts at proselytization by Muslim preachers (*mubalig*) (Timorese orphans were sometimes sent to Java to be brought up in Islamic boarding schools [*pesantrèn*]), and the gap between the rhetoric and reality of the much-vaunted Indonesian 'development' (*pembangunan*) policies in terms of the availability of job opportunities for young Timorese, all helped to radicalize the younger generation and ensure their support for the resistance. Even those who had backed integration in 1975–76 as 'the most realistic option' had begun to execrate it by the late 1980s. 'What we have got now is military occupation not integration', complained the politically moderate head of the East Timor Agricultural Development Program (ETADEP), Florentino Sarmento, a Timorese educated partly under the Portuguese, partly under the Indonesians. 'Access to social and political rights has been denied. [Indonesian policies in East Timor] are spreading the seeds of disintegration. It's very paradoxical.' 'For us all Timorese are Xanana. If one Xanana is captured, another Xanana will come' was the more radical response of those prepared to move up to the mountains to carry on the fight in the face of the later capture (20 November 1992) of the revered guerrilla leader.

As the student resistance began to develop into what might be termed a Timorese 'intifada' during the course of the 1980s, its importance to the wider resistance movement was immediately recognized by the Falintil guerrillas in the mountains. In his conversations with Domm, Xanana spoke of the 'great significance' of the younger generation for the future of the nationalist struggle in Timor, and explained how even secondary school children (from Class 3 upwards) were participating in clandestine organizations. One of these was Donaciano Gomes (born 1969), who was later to be one of the student organizers of the pro-independence demonstration at the time of Pope John Paul II's visit to Timor on 12 October 1989 and who was subsequently detained and tortured by the Indonesians before being allowed to leave the country for exile in Portugal. He recalled:

In 1983–84, when I was fourteen years old, I became directly involved in the conflict because I could no longer bear the barbarous actions of the Indonesian [military] who were massacring people day and night, imprisoning them without pretext, and violating women as they pleased. What meaning did these actions have? For me, growing up in East Timor was a deeply tragic experience. It was [at this time] in 1983–84 that I met someone who had become a member of the guerrilla resistance while living in a village. He was later captured by the Indonesians, subjected to terrible torture, and then sent as a political prisoner to Atauro Island. He was dead within a year. Naturally I was influenced by these events – who could not have been? (Peter Carey and G. Carter-Bentley [eds.], *East Timor at the Crossroads: The Forging of a Nation*, [London: Cassell, 1995], pp.106–7)

One key aspect of both this student *'intifada'* and the armed resistance was their link with the Timorese Catholic Church. Forged initially in the bonds which developed between the handful of priests who, like Father Leoneto do Rego, went with Fretilin to the mountains in 1975–76, and the populations in the guerrilla zones, it had developed by the late 1980s into a deep and many-sided relationship, which provided an essential moral dimension to the nationalist struggle. This was stressed by Xanana who spoke of the way in which the clergy 'had played an indirect role, strengthening patriotic consciousness', so that 'the people had [developed] an enormous trust in the Catholic Church. They feel that it isn't isolated from their suffering, but in solidarity with them. Many priests have been threatened with shooting [by the Indonesian military] . . .'

This trust between clergy and people had been deepened by the feeling of isolation and abandonment experienced by the Timorese religious in the face of the seeming indifference of the wider Catholic Church. In 1981, in a *Reflection* addressed to the religious orders in Indonesia, the Timorese priests spoke bitterly of the failure of the Catholic Church in Indonesia and the Central Roman Church to 'state openly and officially their solidarity with the Church, people and religious of East Timor. Perhaps this has been the heaviest blow for us [. . . .] We felt stunned by this silence, which seemed to allow us to die deserted.' Conscious of its obligations to the nearly 5,000,000-strong Catholic community in Indonesia proper, the Vatican had always shown itself reluctant to speak too openly about Timor for fear of jeopardizing its relations with Jakarta. Thus, while it did not recognize Indonesia's annexation – the official Vatican line was that Timor 'had freed itself from Portugal but had not yet joined Indonesia' – and was willing to stress the need 'for consideration to be given in every circumstance to the ethnic, religious and cultural identity of the [Timorese] people', it was not prepared to condemn Indonesian human rights abuses or push for a genuine act of self-determination in the territory. When Mgr. Martinho da Costa Lopes (in office, May 1977–May 1983), the outspoken Timorese Apostolic Administrator, began openly to criticize Indonesian actions, especially the massacre at Lacluta to the southeast of Dili in September 1981 in which 400 people, mostly women and children, were dashed to death against rocks and trees, the Vatican bowed to pressure from Jakarta to get rid of him (he later died in exile in Lisbon in February 1991 'of neglect and a broken heart').

His replacement, Mgr. Carlos Filipe Ximenes Belo (b. 1948), a young Timorese Salesian priest, who had only recently returned to Timor from Rome to serve as Director of Fatumaca College, was thought initially by Jakarta and the Vatican to be more biddable. But they were soon proven wrong when Belo showed that he was just as opposed to Indonesian actions as his predecessor. Already in December 1984, he was writing that 'despite all the forces against us, we continue to hold [. . .] that the only solution to the Timor conflict is a political and diplomatic one, and this should include, above all, the respect for the right of a people for self-determination.' ('East Timor, An international Responsibility', *Comments*. [London: CIIR, 1992], pp. 28–29).

The following year, he was even bolder, putting his name to a public *Statement* by the Timorese Council of Priests addressed to the Indonesian authorities which warned explicitly of the threat of ethnocide in East Timor: '[The] attempt to Indonesianise the Timorese people through vigorous campaigns to promote *pancasila*, through schools or the media, by alienating the people from their world view, means the gradual murder of Timorese culture. To kill the culture is to kill the people'. Although he was forced on this occasion to repudiate his signature, he was later to return to the fray with his December 1987 pastoral letter, in which he accused the Indonesian military of 'regularly practising torture'. But it was his private letter to the UN Secretary-General (then Sr Perez de Cuellar) in February 1989, which stressed that 'the people of East Timor must be allowed to express their views on their future through a plebiscite', which aroused the most violent response from the Indonesian authorities. This time he stood firm, even making his position more explicit by stating that he was not advocating one political solution over another, but affirming a basic principle. His courage in the face of numerous threats, including two attempted assassinations (in 1989 and 1991) – he has long warned that he may go the way of Archbishop Oscar Romero, the Salvadorian Church leader gunned down in 1980 while saying mass – has been an inspiration for many Timorese, and a living affirmation of the solidarity between Church and people.

This solidarity is especially noticeable in the way in which the Church has cared for the wives, widows, children and orphans of the Timorese resistance fighters. This has been done principally through the institution of the *colégios*, Catholic centres consisting of a parish church, a convent for priests, lay brothers and nuns, a boarding school for boys or girls, and a large tract of agricultural land, usually partly rented out to local farmers and partly cultivated by the students themselves to grow food for their school kitchen. Venilale, the once elegant Portuguese town built on the northern-western escarpment of Mount Matebian near Baucau, is the site of one such *colégio*, where the children and orphans of *guerrilheiros* are looked after. When Norman Lewis visited there in 1992, Xanana's wife, Justina, and her two young children (one the offspring of a forced union with her Indonesian prison guard after her surrender), were in residence, along with 200 other boys and girls between the ages of two and twelve. With many suffering from malaria and tuberculosis due to poor diet and their years spent on the run in the forest with their parents, most of whom were now either dead or in prison, the nuns had to act as nurses, mothers, teachers and sisters all rolled into one. But what immediately impressed was the loving energy with which these roles were accomplished. Here was the striking Filipina nun, the 32-year-old Sister Marlene, in her austere Salesian habit, who had struggled through the thickets of Soul Mountain to bring succour to children under attack from the air during the terrible 1977–78 encirclement and annihilation campaign, breaking into a vigorous Portuguese folk-dance with a class of young orphan girls; here was the Italian Sister Paola Battagliola, with her tiny triangular face of the Neapolitan witch-fairy *'a buffona*, carrying out all the domestic tasks, including the management of the kitchen, with 'a miracle of efficiently applied effort'. Amid all the organized evil of the Indonesian occupation, they shone forth like stars in a jet-black sky. Fortunate indeed were the children in their care – amid the tens of thousands of orphans in Timor, they at least would know the meaning of love.

This network of *colégios* and Church centres caring for the families of resistance fighters, also played an interesting role in keeping alive a knowledge of Portuguese language and customs. For a younger Timorese generation denied access to such knowledge in Indonesian schools and a latter-day colonial society dominated by the alien culture of inner-island Indonesia, especially Java, the Timorese Church offered a unique cultural space. Here not only was the Lusophone inheritance of the pre-1975 era honoured, but respect was also shown for pre-Christian Timorese belief systems, the local veneration for *lulik* (heirlooms) and the empowering energy of the cockerel dance in which the young male dancers under the guidance of a shaman take on the elemental vitality of fighting cocks. 'These people are godly in a truly religious sense', a nun explained to Lewis in Venilale, 'we have learnt to co-exist with their animism.' Watching the pagan symbols of the moon displayed in full view of the cross during the dance celebration at the time of Bishop Belo's visit to Venilale, Lewis concluded that 'here the Church was prepared to show not merely tolerance in its handling of shamanistic competition, but had [actually] sided with it in the face of government disfavour.' Indeed, the iconography of the Catholic Church with its crucifixes, statues of the Blessed Virgin, grottos and *via dolorosa* structures soon came to serve as substitutes for the multifarious forms of ancestor worship and *lulik* veneration which had become increasingly difficult to carry out in Timor because of their potential association with Fretilin gatherings.

Portuguese, previously the language of oppression in the colonial era, was now rapidly transformed into the language of resistance. Abolished from public and private schools in the early 1980s, along with its use in the liturgy, it had become, by the late 1980s, the vehicle of clandestine communication *par excellence* between the resistance leaders and student militants both in East Timor and abroad, as well as in Timorese Church circles. At the same time, Tetun had taken its place as the popular language of Timorese national identity, a *lingua franca* which had condemned most other Timorese vernacular languages, of which there had been about a dozen before the Indonesian invasion, to near extinction. Curiously, the Indonesian policy of forcing all the surrendered Timorese populations into 'resettlement camps' after the 1977–78 encirclement had hastened this process of linguistic unification, for Tetun had now to be used as the language of communication between the very diverse populations in the camps, many of whom hailed from different parts of the country and could no longer rely on intercourse with their own ethnic communities. In this fashion, the Indonesians, whose educational system only inculcated a working knowledge of *Bahasa* in a relatively small proportion of the school-age population at this time, inadvertently contributed to the growth of a language of Timorese national unity.

The 'opening' of East Timor and the background to the Santa Cruz Massacre (1989–91)

Surveying the developments in East Timor during the 1980s, the Indonesian authorities may have begun to feel that the worst was over – the trauma of the encirclement and annihilation campaign of the late 1970s had led to the destruction of Falintil as a conventional army. True, there was still guerrilla resistance, particularly in the seven most easterly districts of the island between Baucau, Viqueque and Lospalos, but this seemed to be containable through the adoption of increasingly sophisticated counter-insurgency tactics and the rapid 'Timorization' of the war. The size of this armed resistance remained small, and, by their own admission, incapable of winning striking victories. It also seemed that the massive resettlement of the highland populations after the fall of Mount Matebian in December 1978 had broken the back of the civilian support for the guerrillas. The inexorable march of Indonesian-inspired 'progress', especially the massive primary-school building programme, looked set to win at least the new generation of Timorese to the Indonesian side and ensure support for integration in the 1990s. Then, perhaps, Jakarta might allow itself the luxury of a 'plebiscite' which would prove once and for all the finality of East Timor's incorporation as the Republic's 27th Province.

How much the Indonesian intelligence community knew about the subterranean currents which were even then transforming the nationalist struggle in East Timor is unclear. Just before his death in 1984, it is known that Moertopo decided to test public opinion in East Timor by sending in Indonesian artisans to work alongside Timorese on building sites and government development projects to sound out local opinion regarding the likely outcome of such a referendum. When almost entirely negative reports began to flow back about the political attitudes of ordinary Timorese, the idea of a plebiscite was promptly shelved. It would not be taken up again until the 1990s, when the rapid inflow of migrants from inner-island Indonesia had begun to affect a profound alteration in Timor's demographic balance.

Internationally, pressures on Indonesia had steadily lessened in the 1980s. The last General Assembly debate on East Timor (which had resulted in a narrow vote [50–46] against Indonesia) had taken place in 1982. The following year, on Norway's initiative, further debates had been postponed to allow space for the UN Secretary-General to 'use his good offices' to bring the ongoing talks between Portugal, Indonesia and Fretilin to a successful conclusion. This was the time of the general ceasefire (March–August 1983) between Fretilin and the local Indonesian commander in Dili, Colonel Purwanto, and it seemed that substantive progress might at last be able to be made towards a political solution of the Timor problem. True, Portugal, under the new presidency of Lieutenant-General António dos Santos Ramalho Eanes (in office, 1982–86), was pressing the issue with more vigour than hitherto and his country's admission to full EC membership in January 1986 greatly enhanced Lisbon's influence over Western European diplomacy towards Indonesia on the Timor issue. But even here, the larger European states, especially Britain and West Germany, were very reluctant to jeopardize their burgeoning economic links with Jakarta. Britain was by this time well on the way to becoming Indonesia's largest foreign armaments supplier (it eventually overtook the United States in 1993), providing a whole range of sophisticated weapons' systems – including Hawk ground-attack aircraft (the first contract with British Aerospace had been signed in April 1978) – some of which would later be deployed in East Timor. Elsewhere, support for Jakarta from its key trade partners – Japan and the United States – remained solid, and Australia even accorded *de jure* recognition to Indonesia's annexation in December 1978, the only Western country to take this extraordinary step. The temptation of the oil wealth in the 'Timor Gap' between the former Portuguese colony and Australia, supposedly one of the twenty-five largest oil fields in the world (an estimated 5 billion barrels – three times Australia's current reserves) proved crucial here, Canberra's recognition immediately paving the way to negotiations with Jakarta. These eventually resulted in the 10 December 1989 'Timor Gap' treaty dividing the area into different exploitation zones, a treaty now the subject of a legal dispute between Portugal and Australia at the International Court of Justice in The Hague.

With Indonesia now taking a more aggressive stance in international fora – intensive lobbying by its diplomats secured the removal of East Timor from the agenda of both the UN Human Rights Commission and the Non-Aligned Movement (NAM) in the mid-1980s – and Portugal rediscovering its principles (the new Social Democrat Prime Minister, Aníbal Cavaco Silva, had sided firmly with the Portuguese President [post-March 1986, Mário Soares] in calling for East Timor's 'inalienable right to self-determination'), the UN-brokered talks between Indonesia and Portugal made little headway. The only decision of substance to emerge was the agreement to allow a Portuguese Parliamentary delegation to visit East Timor to make a report on the situation to the government in Lisbon with an eye to shaping a final political settlement. Although this decision was reached in principle in 1988, nearly three years were to elapse before the practical arrangements for such a visit could be worked out. Its cancellation at the eleventh hour in early November 1991 was to lead directly to the tragedy of the 12 November Santa Cruz massacre.

In mid-June 1988, when East Timor's Governor, Mário Viegas Carrascalão (in office, September 1982 – September 1992), asked President Suharto to 'open' East Timor and allow it to be treated like any other Indonesian province, the shadow of Santa Cruz still lay far in the future. Carrascalão, a Portuguese-trained agricultural engineer and scion of a wealthy *mestiço* family from Baucau with interests in coffee, had worked hard during his governorship to develop Timor and speed the process of economic reconstruction after the trauma of the late 1970s. One of the founding members of UDT, along with his brother João (who later went into exile in Australia and supported the Timorese Resistance Front [CNRM]), he was no stranger to the troubled politics of Timor. But he held fast to the belief that properly directed development policies – particularly the provision of jobs for the growing numbers of educated young Timorese – together with a gradual demilitarization of the province, would ultimately ensure a peaceful future for the territory. Although viewed in some resistance circles as an unprincipled collaborator, he was a genuinely sincere man who had the interests of his country at heart. His misfortune was that he consistently overestimated the capacity of the Indonesians – particularly the military – to think and act creatively in the Timor context. Their minds continued to run on fixed tracks with security concerns and the imperatives of the 'Indonesianization' process outweighing the deeper values of local empowerment and culturally-appropriate development. Thus, although Carrascalão succeeded in convincing Jakarta of the need to end Timor's closed status – the territory (apart from the eastern districts where fighting was still continuing) was officially 'opened' by Presidential Decree at the end of December 1988 and put on a par with other Indonesian regions – the consequences of this decision were far from universally beneficial for the Timorese people. In fact, it lit a powder trail which was eventually to explode at Santa Cruz.

One immediate consequence of the 'opening' was the rapid influx of newcomers from Sulawesi, the province of Nusa Tenggara Timur (NTT), and inner-island Indonesia (Java, Bali and Madura), into Timor. Carrascalão had in part foreseen this, but he had expected that the benefits of allowing the Timorese population to travel freely both within the territory and outside (previously all such movement had required special security clearance), and the inflow of private investment – with its potential for local job creation – would counterbalance the negative effects of unrestricted migration. He was wrong. Because of fears about the security situation and the existence of powerful military-linked commercial monopolies, private investors were reluctant to put their money into Timor. In the three years following the 'opening' slightly over US$1 million was pledged (for the development of fisheries, seaweed processing, and travel agencies), about what the Indonesian government was supposed to have been spending a day on the war in the mid-1980s. Even investment linked to the development of the 'Timor Gap' oil field had not materialized by the early 1990s, the decision having been taken to favour Darwin, Jakarta and Kupang (West Timor) over the interests of Suai, the most proximate port on East Timor's south coast. Again security considerations may have played a part, the south coast still being within range of Timorese guerrillas operating from the mountains.

The presence of well-entrenched commercial monopolies operated by the military had long been a feature of the Indonesian occupation. Shortly after the December 1975 invasion, a Chinese businessman linked to the key officers in the East Timor campaign – Major-General Murdani (then a senior officer in military intelligence), Brigadier-General Dading Kalbuadi (first military commander [*Panglima*] in Timor) and Colonel (later General) Adolf Sahala Rajagukguk (later head of the East Timor military district, 1979–82) – had set up a firm, PT Denok Hernandes International. This quickly became the territory's dominant enterprise with a monopoly over coffee purchases (Timorese growers were forced to accept prices well below the going market rate), sandalwood (exploited virtually to exhaustion by the late 1980s), marble (a local handicraft now largely in the hands of Javanese migrants), and sugar. By the time of Timor's 'opening' in 1989, PT Denok had become part of an even larger army-controlled conglomerate, PT Batara Indra, with interests in real estate, freight, tourism, entertainment, civil engineering, and import/export. It is thus understandable that private investors found few openings in East Timor for it remained to all intents and purposes a commercial fief of the Indonesian army. Cynics even suggested that the tardiness with which the military went about the business of apprehending the Timorese resistance leader, Xanana, had more than a little to do with their economic interests: 'The Indonesian army will never leave,' one Italian priest observed, '[for] if Xanana dies or is captured, they will have to invent another resistance leader. They are making so much money here!'

The economic activities of the Indonesian army in East Timor were camouflaged by the showy conceit of 'development' (*pembangunan*). 'We have done more for East Timor in twenty years than the Portuguese did in four-and-a-half centuries' has been the refrain of Indonesian officials charged with defending their country's record in the former Portuguese colony. Indeed, *pembangunan* has been a shibboleth of Suharto's 'New Order', the President's proudest title being that of '*Bapak Pembangunan*' ('Father of Development'), accorded him in the early 1980s when Indonesia's economic transformation from the chaos of the mid-1960s had become plain for all to see. In the case of East Timor, Jakarta has always pointed to its development record to disarm its Western critics, and pre-empt too close an enquiry into its non-existent legal claim to the territory. Even the army has got in on the act, involving its soldiers in local development schemes under the much trumpeted '*moris diak*' (territorial operation) programme, 'security' now (post-1989) supposedly taking second place to 'welfare'.

At first glance, the achievements look impressive. Between 1976 and 1992, Indonesia spent somewhere in the region of US$750 million (around US$1000 for every man, woman and child currently living in East Timor) on development projects, with particularly large sums going to infrastructure and administrative facilities. By 1991, the pitiful 30 kilometres of asphalt road left by the Portuguese had been increased over tenfold (with a further 2000 kilometres of gravel and dirt highway), and numbers enrolled in secondary education expanded fifty times (to over 50,000), with a dramatic fall in illiteracy rates (from 90 per cent in 1972 to 52 per cent in 1990). No visitor could fail to notice the rows of gleaming new provincial government buildings, quarters for the burgeoning Indonesian civil service; nor the corrugated iron roofs of the ubiquitous military barracks, from where the 15,000-strong Indonesian garrison maintained its guard on the troubled territory.

On deeper inspection, however, much of this 'development' had more to do with the security requirements of the army and the demands of the local administration, than with the needs of the local Timorese population. During the period of the Indonesian Fourth Five-Year Development Plan (1983–89), for example, transport (road building) and local government expenses absorbed close on 50 per cent of the US$270 million spent in the province, with health, education and culture – supposedly top priorities in the Plan – accounting for less than 7 per cent. Even agriculture, the sector which employed the vast bulk (83 per cent) of the Timorese work force, received less than 10 per cent. It was perhaps no surprise that the best roads had been built in the eastern part of the country, where fighting was still taking place, whereas those in the more peaceful western districts were again in a deplorable state by the early 1990s.

The quality of the education and health care provided for the Timorese also left much to be desired. Indonesian teachers and doctors, most of them recently qualified, were poorly motivated and regarded Timor as a hardship post. The ratio between teachers and students at the secondary level was the worst in the whole country, and the number of inhabitants without adequate reading and writing skills was by 1990 still nearly four times the Indonesian national average. At the same time, the best hospitals were reserved for the military or for Indonesian civil servants, Timorese having to make do with poorly equipped civilian facilities or 'people's health centres' (*Puskesmas*) where the exigencies of the government family planning programme, especially the extensive use of the controversial drug Depo-Provera (an injectable contraceptive given to over 65 per cent of all Timorese women 'acceptors' in 1990–91), eclipsed the treatment of more pressing ailments such as malaria, TB and dengue fever. After the 1977–78 'encirclement and annihilation' campaign, there had been cases of Timorese women 'losing' their new-born babies in these Indonesian-staffed hospitals and clinics, and many preferred to use the services of traditional midwives and healers. Indeed, Timorese medicine, based on an extensive knowledge of the curative properties of local plants, continued to thrive despite – perhaps even because of – the existence of this Indonesian-run healthcare 'system'.

The most disappointing feature of the whole Indonesian development programme for the Timorese was undoubtedly its failure to create new jobs for the burgeoning local workforce. This was compounded by the arrival of thousands of 'newcomers' from Indonesia proper, who, by the early 1990s, made up nearly a fifth of the 750,000-strong population, and who appeared to be privileged over the indigenous population in terms of job opportunities.

As we have seen, Jakarta's transmigration programme, which brought hundreds of Balinese and Javanese farmers to sites near the Indonesian border (Maliana and Covalima) and spurred a rush of 'spontaneous' transmigrants from Atambua (Belu district) in West

Timor, created major environmental problems. The generation of land disputes was particularly worrying here: unlike transmigration sites in South Sumatra, Indonesian Borneo (Kalimantan), and Western New Guinea (Irian Jaya), where new agricultural land had been painstakingly carved out of primary jungle, savannah, and marshlands, the ricefields made available on the Maliana plain had been 'acquired' from the local owners without so much as a cent in compensation. The attempt by Jakarta in 1991 to bring landownership law in Timor into line with the practice in other parts of Indonesia, further exacerbated this problem since it seemed that traditional land rights, especially over customary (*adat*) land, would not be recognized. At the same time, the takeover by the army-dominated PT Batara Indra conglomerate of large estates (*fazenda*) previously owned by rich *mestiço* families or the Portuguese (eg the SAPT [*Sociedade Agricóla Pátria e Trabalho*] enterprise which engaged in coffee growing and export) greatly increased the problems of absentee landownership, environmental degradation (destruction of sandalwood forests), and conflicts with local Timorese farmers. The promise of land-reform and land redistribution raised earlier during the brief Fretilin interregnum of the mid-1970s now seemed increasingly remote.

Writing in 1990, an Indonesian government-sponsored study of the 'impact of integration' spoke ominously of the deep divisions which had opened up in Timorese society and warned of the danger of social unrest. The deepest of these cleavages undoubtedly affected East Timorese youth, particularly the 50,000 secondary school students, and those 1000 or more who had studied at the territory's two technical colleges (at Dili and Fatumaca) or who had been to universities in inner Indonesia since the mid-1980s. Their resentment at the non-Timorese newcomers – the so-called Battalion 702 (the numbers referring to their leaving for work early in the morning [7], not bringing any benefit to the local economy [0], and then going home in the afternoon [2]), was particularly intense. The Makasarese and Buginese from South Sulawesi, who had by the early 1990s begun to engross nearly all the retail trade in Dili and other important towns, were viewed as especially extortionate. 'What's the good of school if there's no way of getting a decent job?', one Timorese secondary school student from Gleno put it, 'These days [1990] all office jobs are closed to us. If the Regional Office Head [*Kakanwil*] in a [local government] department is a newcomer, he will only be interested in having his relatives, or at least people from the same region as him, working in his office.'

Throughout the late 1980s, the number of East Timorese job seekers unable to be absorbed into a workforce now dominated by 'newcomers' continued to rise. Whereas 21 per cent had got jobs in 1983, by 1987, only 3.4 per cent of the estimated 4707 job seekers found paid employment. The total number of new employment opportunities created by the whole of the Indonesian Fourth Five-Year Development Plan (1983–89) was a pitiful 1675, just under 4 per cent of what would have been necessary to find jobs for all school leavers during that period. Neither private companies nor local government were able to absorb this new generation of bright and educated young Timorese. Indeed, the fact that the monopolistic practices of the military-dominated companies had effectively 'closed off' whole sectors of the modern economy to East Timorese school leavers and graduates led them to question the relevance of educational institutions for their future. At the same time, their mastery of Indonesian had given them access to a world beyond Timor and Indonesia, much in the same fashion that the Dutch had given Indonesian intellectuals access to a world beyond the Netherland East Indies during the period of Indonesian national 'awakening' (*jaman kebangkitan nasional*) at the turn of the century.

Of particular importance here were the contacts which had begun to be forged between East Timorese students in Indonesian universities with Indonesian academics and members of non-governmental organizations (NGOs), who themselves were now starting to assess the limits of Indonesian nationalism and who had become increasingly convinced that the East Timor issue should be placed much higher up the domestic agenda. Some even argued for a proper referendum on the country's political future. In this fashion, just as Dutch liberals had questioned the rightness of Dutch authority in colonial Indonesia before 1945, a handful of educated Indonesians had begun the dangerous debate on the legitimacy of Indonesian rule in East Timor in the 1990s.

These debates as yet found little resonance in government circles, where belief in the rectitude of Indonesia's East Timor policy ruled supreme. If the initial Indonesian invasion and occupation had recalled fourteenth-century Majapahit, Jakarta's 'education-repression-development' strategies in East Timor in the 1980s and early 1990s now cast it in the role of the latter-day Netherland Indies colonial state. 'Look at all we have done for you. Where is your gratitude?' The accusatory words of Dili-based Indonesian officials towards their 'ungrateful' East Timorese charges might have tripped off the tongue of any member of the Dutch *Binnenlandsch Bestuur* (colonial administration) when faced with the intransigence of the early Indonesian nationalists. Unfortunately, history, apart from the most ersatz *'pancasila'* variety taught in their academies and staff colleges, had never been the Indonesian military's forte. Lacking any reflective capacity, the only response they knew was kneejerk violence. So the stage was set for the tragedy of Santa Cruz and the shattering of colonial illusions.

The Santa Cruz Massacre (12 November 1991) and its aftermath

Long before the 12 November 1991 Santa Cruz massacre, there had been abundant evidence that the situation in East Timor was heading for a showdown between the Indonesian military and the student-led Timorese *intifada*. Already, in the first year of the territory's 'opening', public demonstrations against integration had taken place at the time of Pope John Paul II's visit on 12 October 1989 (the fact that Taci-Tolu, once an Indonesian detention centre and execution ground outside Dili, had been chosen by the Indonesian authorities as the site for the papal mass added a particular poignancy to this protest), and during US Ambassador John Monjo's brief stay in Dili on 17 January 1990. Later that year, on 4 September, on the occasion of the fiftieth anniversary celebration of the establishment of the diocese of Dili, another student-organized anti-integration event occurred, which, like the others, sparked off a wave of Indonesian arrests, with many young people being subjected to periods of torture and imprisonment.

One of these was Donaciano Gomes, who took refuge in Bishop Belo's residence after the papal mass protest and eventually surrendered himself to the Indonesian military commander, Brigadier-General Mulyadi, along with several other activists, when the commander promised that they would not be ill-treated but would be released after a short interrogation. Instead, he was tortured for fifteen long days by Indonesian special forces (*Kopassus*) with cigarette burns, electric shocks, blows to the head and gun muzzles pointed at his head, chest and mouth in an attempt to get him to implicate a Spanish priest as one of the instigators of the demonstration. Among those involved in the interrogation of student demonstrators at this time was the newly promoted Lieutenant-Colonel Prabowo, Suharto's son-in-law, now back in East Timor on another tour of duty (such tours being especially beneficial for military career prospects), who personally broke the leg and teeth of one of Donaciano Gomes's friends, Idelfonso Araujo. Nearly four months were to pass before Gomes was released, and another seven before he could finally leave Timor for exile in Portugal. So much for Indonesian promises and the word of honour of its officers.

Important though these demonstrations were in signalling the coming of age of a new resistance generation in Timor, it was the news that the long-awaited Portuguese parliamentary delegation would at last visit the territory in November 1991, which concentrated minds in the latter part of that year. Quite unrealistic expectations were attached to this visit on both the Indonesian and Timorese sides. For the Indonesians, there were hopes that the visit would open the way for a political settlement with Portugal which would lay the Timor issue to rest once and for all; for the Timorese, there was a belief that the arrival of the Portuguese would lead to a new resolve in Lisbon to finish the decolonization process so tragically interrupted in August 1975, and put pressure on Jakarta to accept an internationally-supervised referendum. With such pent-up emotions ready to burst forth, Dili awaited confirmation of the delegation's arrival. It never came. During the discussions between the Portuguese and the Indonesians over the practical arrangements for the visit, Jakarta made objections to the inclusion of a Lisbon-based Australian journalist and long-time Timor watcher, Jill Jolliffe, in the accompanying Portuguese press group. This was unacceptable to Lisbon, Indonesia having earlier indicated that the choice of media personnel would not be subject to special restriction. So, in late October, the visit was cancelled.

In Timor, the effect was electric. So much store had been set by this visit and so many preparations made (old Portuguese flags searched out, Fretilin banners and ensigns sewn, and posters – in Portuguese and English – proclaiming East Timor's inalienable right to self-determination designed) that a cancellation of the planned demonstrations was unthinkable. There had already been violent clashes between the Indonesian security forces and the student activists, which had resulted in the deaths of a young man, Sebastião Gomes, and a Timorese member of a *ninja* (masked killer) unit which had broken into the Motael Church in Dili at 2.30 in the morning of 28 October to harass the sheltering students. This sparked a huge protest, in which nearly half the population of Dili took part. Despite Indonesian arrests and intimidation, large numbers turned out again the following day (29 October) to accompany Sebastião's funeral cortege to the Santa Cruz cemetery. Then came the news of the cancellation. Despair and desperation overwhelmed every heart. How could the Portuguese fail them yet again? O! Perfidious power to deal so miserably with your martyred children!

But then, a fierce cold courage banished irresolution. What more have we got to lose? Let us show the world that Timor will not be daunted! *Pátria ou Morte*! The demonstrations planned for the Portuguese would go ahead, but in a different setting (up to now there is still much debate about the role of the Indonesian army and its *agents provocateurs* [*bufo*] in turning to tragedy what the Gomes family hoped would remain a peaceful and dignified act of remembrance – the UN Special Rapporteur on Extrajudicial, Summary or Arbitrary Executions would later speak of it as a 'planned military operation' in his 1 November 1994 report). So the day of Timor's destiny dawned: Tuesday, 12 November 1991. As the sun rose over Dili, Fr Ricardo, a Timorese priest prepared to say mass at the Motael Church as hundreds began to gather to take communion before the planned procession to strew flowers on Sebastião's grave and hold a memorial service. Many had posters and flags rolled up inside their clothes. At 7 a.m., the procession, banners now unfurled and waving in the air, moved off along the waterfront, past the grey Indonesian warships lying at anchor. Most were students and young people. As they walked, others joined them from huts and from offices. Some were weeping, but others were smiling and glancing round in astonishment as the chant of *Viva Timor Leste*! [Long Live East Timor!]' pierced the morning air, taunting the Indonesian police and soldiers watching bemused from their barracks. Two to three thousand-strong, the crowd now covered the whole road as it moved briskly to Santa Cruz just a mile distant. So charged were the younger marchers that some broke into a jog, having to be restrained by the older youths and the organizers with loud hailers at the front. '*Disciplina*! [Order!]' – 'Get back in line!' – '*Disciplina*! [Order!]' The gates of the cemetery loomed ahead. The Gomes family went inside followed by young girls with trays of flowers. Some of the marchers climbed on top of the gate and on to the high walls to spread out their flags and banners: 'Tears, Injustice – This is what we suffer!'; '*Xanana Gusmão – Símbolo de União Nacional* [Xanana Gusmão – Symbol of National Unity!]'; '*Viva Falintil*! [Long Live Falintil!]'. Arms raised in salute, the other marchers swarmed around the gate waiting to file into the cemetery, as the march organizers announced that prayers would shortly begin for the deceased. For many, death was just seconds away.

Few saw the army truck pull up to block off the end of the cemetery street, nor heard the column of 200 fully-armed troops as it moved up the road from the town. Marching slowly, the soldiers turned into the cemetery entrance, US-supplied M16 automatic rifles at the ready. Urged on by their civilian-clad officers, the batik-shirted intelligence lieutenant (and torturer), Iswanto, to the fore, they took up firing positions. 'The Gestapo!' Someone had noticed. Terror began to sweep the crowd. Some tried to move away. Too late! They were trapped! The high walls of the cemetery and the narrow encircling streets hemmed them in. Sirens wailing, a sustained volley of automatic fire poured into the crowd – thousands of rounds cutting a swathe of death as people fought desperately to get through the cemetery gate. 'The scene [here] . . . was frozen into my mind', recalls Max Stahl, a British journalist who filmed the massacre from inside the cemetery.

A young man badly wounded, but still not dead, lay across the entrance. Others had tripped and fallen in the dirt. A solid wedge of people were stuck in the entrance, pressed from behind by [those] desperate to escape the hail of bullets. Then the wedge broke, and the people poured screaming through the gap, trampling over the bodies, the wounded and the whole alike. [*The Independent on Sunday*, 17 November 1991].

As a second volley rang out, the soldiers deployed in ordered ranks to surround the cemetery and move in among the tombstones to search out the wounded, and the survivors. Kicked and belaboured with rifle butts and riot sticks, each person was hauled away to be flung into army trucks, the wounded, dead and dying alike piled together in promiscuous confusion. Among the injured was a New Zealand citizen of Malaysian descent, Kamal Bamadhaj, who had come to Timor as a member of a Sydney-based student solidarity organization. Bleeding profusely from a deep bullet wound in his right chest, he had managed to stagger 500 meters down the street outside the cemetery, before collapsing.

Although the Indonesians had stripped him of all his belongings, he still clutched his New Zealand passport which he waved in a frantic bid to attract help. He was found by the local representative of the International Committee of the Red Cross (ICRC) in Dili and driven, still conscious, towards Dili General Hospital. Despite the Red Cross markings, the Indonesians refused to let the ICRC vehicle pass their road block outside the cemetery, and when he eventually reached the main military hospital forty minutes later, his trauma had been so severe he could not be saved.

If Kamal at least died in hospital surrounded by professional medical care, the Timorese survivors of the massacre were not so fortunate. Outside the cemetery, many had dived for cover as the shooting started. The Indonesians advanced telling all the wounded to stand up. Many of those who did so were cut down with throwing knives. Meanwhile, ten trucks of the dead and dying were dumped at Wira Husada No.4 Military Hospital in Dili. Few of the wounded survived long: some were crushed under the wheels of vehicles in the hospital compound, others stoned to death or forced to swallow paraformaldehyde pills, a lethal disinfectant normally used to kill insects. They died slowly and in agony from internal bleeding and heart attacks. Meanwhile, inside the hospital mortuary, the bodies were piled high 'like a car-load of sand'. Some were still alive, crying out for water and treatment. An Indonesian soldier and hospital orderly moved among them feeding them paraformaldehyde or crushing their heads and chests with rocks. In the early hours of 13 November, all the electricity was switched off in Dili and, under cover of darkness, the bodies were removed, trucked out of the city and dumped in mass graves (already prepared before the aborted Portuguese visit). Then, on 15 November, three days after the massacre, about eighty Timorese, who had been captured after the massacre, were blindfolded, bundled onto army trucks and taken to Bé-Musi, a well-known execution site on the western outskirts of Dili, where they were shot by firing squad.

In all, it is estimated by the Lisbon-based Ecumenical Association, *A Paz é Possível em Timor Leste* (Peace is Possible in East Timor), based on careful analysis of information collected in East Timor between November 1991 and February 1992, that 271 were killed, 250 missing, and 382 wounded. Many of the injured avoided going to hospitals for fear of being arrested, tortured or killed, preferring instead to be treated by relatives or in the Church-run *colégios*, where they were looked after by nuns. Collective and individual massacres continued for many days after 12 November, the last known killing being that of a 13-year-old boy, Gil Vieira Amaral, in Baucau, over 100 kilometres from Dili, on 24 November. Among the 250 missing were 24 members of a single family who lived in the Fatu Hada neighbourhood of Dili.

Massacres on this scale were not unusual in the context of the Indonesian occupation of East Timor: Areia Branca (December 1975), Quelicai (January 1979), Lacluta (September 1981), and Kraras (August 1983), had all formed part of the pattern of systematic violence which underpinned Jakarta's rule in the territory. Yet, this time it was different. There were Western journalists present, two of whom – Steve Cox, whose photographs appear in this volume, and Max Stahl, whose dramatic video footage was later shown around the world – actually filmed the events in the cemetery. It was impossible, given this visual evidence, for the Indonesian authorities to deny that killings had taken place or that the Indonesian army had been involved. But they sought to downplay this by referring to the massacre as a 'regrettable incident' (*musibah*) – shades of the Chinese version of Tiananmen (June 1989) – and only admitting to a fraction of the number of casualties estimated by Timorese and Western observers (the army originally acknowledged 19 dead and 91 wounded, whereas the Indonesian National Commission of Enquiry set up by Suharto in the aftermath of the massacre pushed the number of dead up to 50, and conceded that 'more than 91' might have been wounded).

Indonesian army officers responsible for East Timor operations showed themselves to be completely insensitive to international criticism. General (now Vice-President) Try Sutrisno, Armed Forces Commander-in-Chief, told the Indonesian National Defence Institute (*Lemhanas*) two days after the massacre that '... The [Indonesian] army cannot be underestimated. Finally we had to shoot them. Delinquents like these agitators must be shot, and they will be, whenever necessary . . .', words echoed later by the new commander of the eastern Indonesian military region, which includes Timor, Major-General Mantiri; 'We don't regret anything. What happened was quite proper (*wajar*). [. . .] They were opposing us, demonstrating, even yelling things against the government. To me that is identical with rebellion, so that is why we took firm action' [*Editor* (Jakarta), 4 July 1992]. Indeed, the newly appointed local commander in Timor, Brigadier-General Syafei (in office, 1992–94), admitted on several occasions that his predecessor, Brigadier-General Rudy Warouw, had been too 'soft', and that under him 'there would probably have been more victims'.

In making such statements, the Indonesian military clearly felt that the international reaction to the massacre would be short lived – Indonesia was such an important economic prize and its relations with Western governments so good, that the public outcry in the West seemed somehow irrelevant. The initial response from regional governments appeared to confirm this. One might have expected Wellington to have reacted strongly to the assassination of one of its citizens, but no; besides *pro forma* expressions of 'concern' and the need to 'think carefully' about the massacre, Prime Minister Jim Bolger was quick to reassure Suharto that he would not be cutting military links with Indonesia. It was the same in Australia, where there was little desire to jeopardize bilateral trade ties worth well over US$1 billion a year. Canberra soon signalled that the business of dividing up East Timor's oil wealth would continue as normal when, on 18 December 1991, barely a month after Santa Cruz, it signed a new agreement with Indonesia regulating their 'Joint Authority' in the Timor Gap. It also did its best to prevent pictures of the massacre reaching the West by ordering its immigration officials in Darwin to conduct a rigorous search of the belongings of both Stahl and Cox when they flew out through Northern Australia in late November (fortunately, both had had the presence of mind to entrust their film to reliable couriers, one of whom exited Timor by another route).

So confident were the Indonesian military that no sanctions would be taken against them, that Major-General Sintong Panjaitan, the eastern Indonesian region military commander, who had been 'suspended' after the massacre by an Honorary Military Council, decided to take a sabbatical in the United States ostensibly to enroll in a course at Harvard. Only the threat of a civil action in a local Boston court brought against him by the mother of Kamal Bamadhaj eventually forced him to flee the US in October 1992. Even then his 'disgrace' was short-lived – today he holds a position as adviser to Indonesian Research and Technology Minister, B.J. Habibie, and has been able to ignore the US$14 million damages awarded against him by the US judiciary.

What Jakarta had not bargained for, however, was the sheer scale and durability of the wider international response. At least three Western governments (Canada, Denmark and the Netherlands) suspended their aid programmes to Indonesia, and the US Congress struck Jakarta out of the US$2.4m International Military Education and Training (IMET) facility, a move reinforced in 1994 when Congress barred Indonesia from buying US small arms out of its own funds. This had much to do with the end of the Cold War. Times had changed. Repressive 'security states' like Indonesia could now no longer rely on unquestioning Western support. The fight against communism had been 'won'. In this context, a free East Timor was no longer equated with a Southeast Asian 'Cuba'. Access to natural resources, especially oil, and local markets were now much more important. The International Court of Justice (ICJ) decision on the Indonesian-Australian 'Timor Gap' treaty, expected in mid-1995, is bound to be of special relevance here. A judgement against Australia will have serious implications for future development of the 'Timor Gap' field, and might hasten a settlement of the sovereignty issue which would, of necessity, require a properly supervised act of self-determination in the territory.

The glaring publicity surrounding the massacre and key subsequent events made it increasingly difficult for Jakarta to finesse the East Timor issue in international fora. The obvious discrepancy between the light 8–18 month sentences passed by an Indonesian military court on ten military personnel involved in the shootings, and the harsh punishments (a life sentence in one case) imposed on 21 East Timorese 'ring leaders' of the demonstrations in Dili (28 October), Santa Cruz (12 November) and Jakarta (19 November), all raised questions about the legitimacy of Indonesia's occupation.

Whereas in the mid-1980s, East Timor had slipped off the agenda of the UN Human Rights Commission, the Santa Cruz events placed it back on centre stage. More searching investigations now began to be undertaken into Indonesia's human rights record, and the Kenyan Attorney-General, Amos Wako, dispatched as a personal envoy of the UN Secretary-General to Indonesia and East Timor in early February 1992 to make a report on the massacre (this was never published but, according to private UN sources, its findings were 'horrific'). A year later (10 March 1993), Jakarta suffered an important defeat in the Commission, when a resolution, sponsored by the European Union, expressed its 'deep concern' at reports of continuing human rights abuses in the territory and urged Jakarta to invite four special UN rapporteurs and working groups (an unprecedented number) to Dili to investigate the situation, and report on the 12 November massacre. The decision by the new Clinton Administration (in office, January 1993 to present) to back the resolution, was critical to its success, and signalled an important change in Washington's East Timor policy.

When, eventually, in December 1994, the report of the UN Special Rapporteur on Extrajudicial, Summary or Arbitrary Executions, the Senegalese jurist Bacre Waly N'diaye was released, it amounted to a devastating attack on the Indonesian government, calling for an entirely new investigation into Santa Cruz and making many other recommendations for the improvement of the human rights situation in Timor. This went before the Human Rights Commission in February 1995, and looked set to reinforce moves for another strong resolution against Indonesia. (In the event the Commission adopted a 'consensus statement' which called for a visit to Dili by the UN Human Rights Commissioner.) Pressure is also mounting to allow free access to East Timor by independent human rights organizations like Asia Watch and Amnesty

International, a move which Indonesian Foreign Minister, Ali Alatas, gave incautious justification for in a press briefing at the National Press Club in Washington on 20 February 1992, when he deplored the fact that these organizations had not been available to enquire into human rights violations during the Indonesian revolutionary war against the Dutch (1945–49).

While these initiatives have been taking place in the Commission, talks between Indonesia and Portugal, mandated by the UN General Assembly in 1982 but broken off shortly before Santa Cruz, have been resumed. So far five sessions have taken place under the aegis of the UN Secretary-General, Boutros Boutros-Ghali, the most recent in Geneva in January 1995. Although the core issues of sovereignty and self-determination have yet to be addressed, there has been progress on bringing a broader spectrum of Timorese leaders, both pro- and anti-integrationist, into the 'consultation process'. Already, in January 1994, senior UN officials visited Xanana in prison in Cipinang (Jakarta), and conducted wide-ranging discussions with Bishop Belo and the Timorese clergy in Dili. Despite initial reluctance on the part of Indonesian Foreign Minister, Ali Alatas, to meet Xanana or 'any other Fretilin activists such as Ramos-Horta', it now looks certain that they will be included in future talks. Indeed, the way Jakarta deals with Xanana, in particular whether he is released from prison (where he is serving a twenty-year sentence), will be the clearest signal of its seriousness in coming to a political solution in East Timor. The fiftieth anniversary celebrations of the Indonesian Republic in August 1995 may well be a suitable occasion to announce such a release.

As of the time of writing (January 1995), there are still few signs that Jakarta has made the decision to grasp this political nettle. Reports coming back from Timor indicate that fresh massacres of civilians have taken place in Baucau following ethnic clashes between East Timorese and Bugis traders on 1 January, which resulted in the burning of the main market. The issue of population transfers from Indonesia and settlement in East Timor is now at the top of the agenda, with genuine fears on the Timorese side that Jakarta's long-term policy is to so alter the ethnic balance in Timor, with the influx of thousands of inner-island migrants, that it will eventually so dilute Timorese identity that any plans for autonomous status, or even future independence, would prove impossible of achievement. International pressure on Indonesia to halt any further population transfers is clearly vital in ensuring that talks on East Timor's political future can take place in a less ethnically-charged atmosphere.

The resolution of the East Timor conflict will require statesmanship of a high order and the courage to take unpalatable decisions. Both the Timorese Church, in the person of Bishop Belo, and the CNRM (National Council of Maubere Resistance) have put forward proposals for a settlement which are generous to Indonesia, the first involving a 'special status' for East Timor, a form of autonomy within Indonesia which would begin in the cultural and religious sphere, and then extend to the political and economic realms, resulting in a relationship rather like that of Puerto Rico to the United States, or Madeira and the Azores to Portugal; the second calling for an immediate ceasefire and the release of all political prisoners, followed, within two years, by the reduction of Indonesian troop levels (from the current 17,000 plus) to 1000 and the governance of the territory through a locally elected provincial assembly with Jakarta retaining sovereignty and control of foreign policy, with a properly supervised referendum (with independence as one option) to be held either five or ten years later (the time-scale being decided in Jakarta).

However much it might wish it, Jakarta cannot return to the pre-Santa Cruz era. The 12 November massacre was a watershed as deep in the modern history of East Timor, as the 1962 Sharpeville massacre was in the history of White rule in South Africa. Many years may have to elapse before its full implications become clear, but there can no longer be any pretence that Indonesian-style 'development' is the panacea for all East Timor's problems, or that the fundamental issues of sovereignty and self-determination can be ignored. Jakarta may choose to stick its head in the sand, but the longer it does this the more serious will be the problems which it will store up for itself in terms of the future integrity of its island republic. That integrity has both a political and a moral dimension: politically, Jakarta will have to consider whether its unitary constitution and centralized form of government is the best recipe for success in a far-flung archipelago where the needs of resource-rich outer islands are often in conflict with the resource-deficient (but highly populated) Javanese centre; morally, because, at its heart, the national project begun in Indonesia in the early twentieth century, was grounded in a moral vision of the future. As Radèn Mas Soetomo (1888–1938), one of the founders of that project put it, the true exercise of political freedom requires the development of strong moral and spiritual qualities. Without them, independence (*merdeka*) would be pointless. On the eve of the fiftieth anniversary celebrations of Indonesia's freedom from the Dutch (17 August 1945), and the twentieth anniversary of Fretilin's unilateral declaration of independence (28 November 1975), this is something which both Indonesians and East Timorese would do well to ponder as they prepare for a new relationship in the twenty-first century.

Suggestions for Further Reading

Budiardjo, Carmel and Liem Soei Liong, *The War Against East Timor* (London: Zed Books, 1984) [particularly useful on Fretilin and the nature of the guerrilla war in the early 1980s]

Carey, Peter and G. Carter-Bentley (eds.), *East Timor at the Crossroads: The Forging of a Nation* (London: Cassell, 1995) [collection of essays which cover developments in East Timor from the Portuguese colonial period to the early 1990s. Has an extensive bibliography of works published on East Timor from 1970 to 1994]

Dunn, James, *Timor: A People Betrayed* (Milton, Queensland: The Jacaranda Press, 1983) [the most comprehensive study of the political and diplomatic background to the Indonesian invasion and the first period of East Timorese nationalist struggle, 1975–early 1980s]

Jolliffe, Jill, *East Timor: Nationalism and Colonialism* (St Lucia: University of Queensland Press, 1978) [the best book on the period 1974–76, especially the four-month Fretilin interregnum, September–December 1975, by a journalist who was there]

Lewis, Norman, *An Empire of the East. Travels in Indonesia* (London: Jonathan Cape, 1993) [vividly evokes the situation in East Timor in 1992 through the eyes of a sensitive observer]

Ramos-Horta, José, *Funu. The Unfinished Saga of East Timor* (Trenton, New Jersey: Red Sea Press, 1987) [personal memoir of Fretilin's Special Representative to the UN, particularly useful on the international dimension of East Timor's struggle for independence, 1974–mid-1980s]

Taylor, John G, *The Indonesian Occupation of East Timor, 1974–89. A Chronology* (London: Catholic Institute for International Relations, 1990) [a useful overview of press reports on East Timor during the 1974–89 period]

Taylor, John G, *Indonesia's Forgotten War. The Hidden History of East Timor* (London: Zed Books, 1991) [the most comprehensive coverage of the history of East Timor from the colonial period to the late 1980s]

Turner, Michele, *Telling. East Timor: Personal Testimonies, 1942–92* (Kensington: New South Wales University Press, 1992) [very moving collection of personal testimonies spanning the period from the Australian involvement in World War 2 to the early 1990s]

12 November 1991

The hurried exodus from East Timor by the Portuguese in 1974 and their failure to oversee a smooth transition of power in an established Parliament and Independent Timorese Government, meant that the United Nations still recognized Portugal as the official administrator of East Timor following the Indonesian invasion of the country in 1975.

The reluctance of Western governments to condemn Indonesian actions illustrated the level to which the West was involved with Indonesia. Portugal was a lone voice in Europe fighting a war of words with Jakarta.

Actions speak louder than words as any Timorese will tell you. International indifference has led to the failure of every major foreign delegation to look in depth at the situation in

Above sequence Running through the streets of Dili as the demonstration becomes charged with emotion.

Right Standing on the walls of the cemetery, boys shout passionately for freedom.

57

Arrival at Santa Cruz cemetery.

Boy with Fretilin flag.

Below In East Timor everybody from the youngest to the oldest embraces the right to self-determination.

East Timor. A series of visits arranged between Indonesia and Portugal had all failed and the cancellation at the eleventh hour of yet another proposed visit for 4 November added a further chapter of tragedy to the history of East Timor.

Large-scale demonstrations had been secretly organized throughout the island to confront the delegation, but when the news broke that the visit had been cancelled, a feeling of betrayal and desperation overwhelmed the people. They had suffered needlessly the terror of the military pursuing leaders of the resistance, leaving families torn in half. Those suspected of organizing demonstrations were murdered, tortured or simply disappeared. The sheer desperation of the people, and in particular the young who had borne the brunt of the persecution, made it imperative for some sort of show of defiance. A manifestation had to go ahead in the hope that their struggle for independence would reach the outside world.

At 7am on 12 November 1991 a demonstration left the Motael church after morning mass in protest against Indonesian actions in aborting the Portuguese visit. The demonstrators were aware that their actions would provoke anger and reprisal from the Indonesians. A campaign of terror orchestrated by the Indonesian military prior to the proposed visit by the Portuguese threatened mass executions if anybody made an attempt to approach the delegation. Mass graves were prepared near towns and villages to reinforce this threat. A carefully prepared itinerary and guided tour of the island was arranged, and the command was issued that all buildings, including the smallest of shacks, must fly the Indonesian flag.

Young people spilled out of the church and on to the surrounding roads and months of pent-up frustration and suppressed emotion exploded in the streets as Fretilin banners and flags were unfurled. A feeling of hope and freedom pervaded the crowd in a noisy and excited

Above The streets of Dili.

Left Filing into the cemetery towards the chapel and Sebastião's grave. The cemetery's high walls become a trap as the soldiers surround it.

59

Left and overleaf The killing involves heavily armed soldiers and unarmed protesters. Young people drag themselves into the small chapel where prayers were being said as the massacre began.

atmosphere which created a false expectation as young people ran through the streets shouting for independence. Children as young as eight joined in the procession as it passed schools, bemused Indonesians stared blankly from government buildings, and soldiers scuttled about in the background as other Timorese cheered. The demonstrators became bolder as they passed military posts waving flags depicting their leader, Xanana Gusmão.

As the pace of the demonstration quickened, keeping up with the leading group became increasingly difficult. The march was to pass Santa Cruz cemetery, prayers would be said for Sebastião Gomes who had been killed by soldiers while hiding in the grounds of a church. Cemeteries and churches had become places of refuge for the young victims of nightly purges. The scene at the cemetery was building into a chaotic mass of people as thousands of demonstrators crowded at the gates and boys with banners scaled the high walls surrounding the graveyard shouting '*viva e liberdade*!' As they poured through the gates and headed towards a small chapel, the cry for freedom changed to the sound of prayer. Girls carrying trays of flower petals led a file of people towards the boy's grave. The momentary religious calm became an unnatural hush accompanied by an uneasy shuffling of feet. Moments later, agitation turned to panic

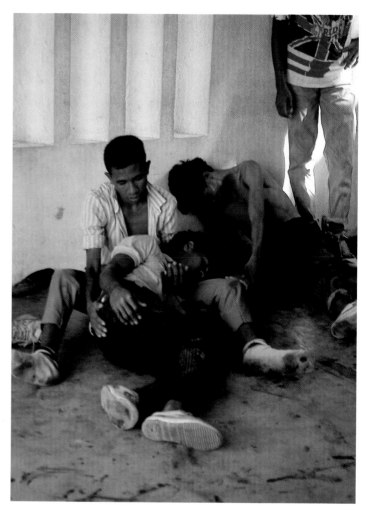

as a tide of terrified people scattered in response to a hail of bullets. The Indonesian military had arrived. Taking up positions around the walls of the cemetery, without warning they began to fire indiscriminately into the crowd.

People took cover, older children shielding the young to protect them as the shooting went on relentlessly. Boys dragged the wounded and dying into the chapel, terror gripped everyone. The Lord's Prayer was repeated with an intensity so charged that it reached fever pitch at the approach of the soldiers as they invaded the cemetery grounds. The killers passed between graves bludgeoning people to death with their rifle butts, hysteria overcame many of the young girls sheltering in the chapel as they saw the soldiers approaching, while others waited silently for

the inevitable end. I will never forget the pitiful sight as I was dragged away, of children cowering in the shadows of the soldiers. It was difficult to comprehend the blood splattered scene as bodies lay in heaps in the dust where only forty minutes earlier several thousand young people had celebrated a taste of freedom.

Some escaped that day but a steady flow of reports that emerged from the island in the following weeks confirmed the subsequent execution of survivors. Witnesses spoke of seeing people lined up around the mass graves and shot.

Despite their attempts to discredit the evidence, the presence of foreign journalists prevented the Indonesian Government from denying the massacre had taken place.

Defying the Occupation

High in the mountainous interior local people describe how they saw rock turn white and trees and scrub disintegrate under rain spewed from military aircraft. The defoliant chemical, Agent Orange, used in Vietnam to such devastating effect by the Americans, has been willingly supplied to Indonesia. Boys from a village in a mountainous part of the country took me to a region where the rock appeared bleached. Being seen with a foreigner can exact a high price and at the approach of a vehicle we lunged for cover in the ditches along the dirt road that led out of the village. Dust billowed from the speeding wheels of military trucks. The mountains were stark and bleak, as black clouds loomed over distant peaks shadowing graveyards that spread out on the horizon. Graves of villagers and unofficial graves of Fretilin fighters littered the landscape as we clambered over white rock to look at hidden tombs.

Young boys in the central mountains of the island.

Opposite A land of crosses is the legacy of Indonesian rule in East Timor. Mass graves are a common sight in most cemeteries.

Human remains in a cave high in the mountains.

Indonesian troops patrolling the outlying area of Lospalos

Ever present eyes keep watch above a cemetery. The grave is of a family killed within the space of three years.

Villagers of Ossu working on the land.

A Timorese youth making placards for the expected Portuguese delegation.

Grandmother and grand-daughter.

Generations of Resistance –wherever you go, young and old alike speak of independence. Integration is a word used with contempt and loathing. Persecution combined with Indonesia's policy of indoctrination has only served to strengthen the resolve of the people to be free and independent. The armed resistance, although small, represents 'Free Timor' and continued hope in the struggle against the Indonesians. Having stood alone, without outside aid or assistance for nearly twenty years, the resistance, drawn from every quarter of society, has held out against integration. The clandestine youth movement is a cohesive force of young people leading an unarmed fight against an armed and brutal aggressor. Families have been slaughtered and their remains scattered under foot; where villages once stood bush has taken over and countless unmarked sites of death riddle the island. Cemeteries are full of mass graves with families annihilated within the space of two to three years, but for each one dead there has always been another to stand and resist. Domingus, a young school teacher, summed up the feelings of the Timorese, 'We are all prepared to sacrifice our lives for freedom, I am the last one of eight brothers and sisters who have all been killed, I will fight for the liberty of my people'. Domingus, who epitomized Timorese determination, died on the 12th of November in Santa Cruz cemetery. Indonesia has failed to indoctrinate the people, particularly the young.

Men of Falintil, the armed resistance. Many of the original men who took to the hills have spent nearly twenty years living in primitive conditions, many in caves. They form a dedicated and highly effective guerrilla operation such as their parents might have formed when they fought with the Allies against the Japanese in the Second World War.

Boys proudly display the flag of Falintil.

Geographically located in the same region as Indonesia, East Timor shares little else in common with the biggest population in South East Asia. Timorese culture and religion is very different in all aspects to the Malay-speaking Indonesians. Even with basics such as food there is a gulf between the cultures. People will tell you of the time when all manner of ingredients were readily available that today are totally absent because the shops are owned by Indonesians.

Above Women and children dancing during a water rites ceremony near Venilale.

Left Timorese girls pounding wheat in a mountain village.

Opposite Women beating gongs at a water rites ceremony on the way to Venilale.

Forcibly made to participate in an annual march past in Dili, Timorese boys were trucked in by the army from outlying areas of the capital to parade alongside the Indonesian armed forces during military parades.

Opposite Lined up with the police, two old women look on as their compatriots perform for the Indonesian authorities.

Forced to perform like circus animals, Timorese were transported by army trucks to Dili from outlying areas to accompany a military parade. Timorese dance and culture were to be displayed alongside the armed forces to demonstrate the notion of a happy integrated Timorese population. A humiliating act as well as an intimidating piece of propaganda, this show was partly for the benefit of a three-man team of international observers who were to witness this spectacle during their visit to Dili. At the prospect of this nauseating experience many of the old men got drunk, adding to the even more absurd sight of villagers dancing to the sound of off-key military bands. All participants were made to wear Indonesian flags as head scarfs or ribbons as they danced in front of high-ranking Indonesian officials and generals outside the Governor's residence. As it turned out, the observers arrived early and missed the parade.

The people were entertained with a 'tug of war' on the day of military parades as different army units pulled against each other.

Timorese wearing Indonesian flags as head scarfs waiting to parade with the military on 5 October 1991.

A Timorese dancer sitting among soldiers during the military parade, Dili, October 1991.

Waiting to dance at the military parade, October 1991.

Opposite Overcome by the heat and circumstance, people collapse during the forced marches that accompanied the military parade.

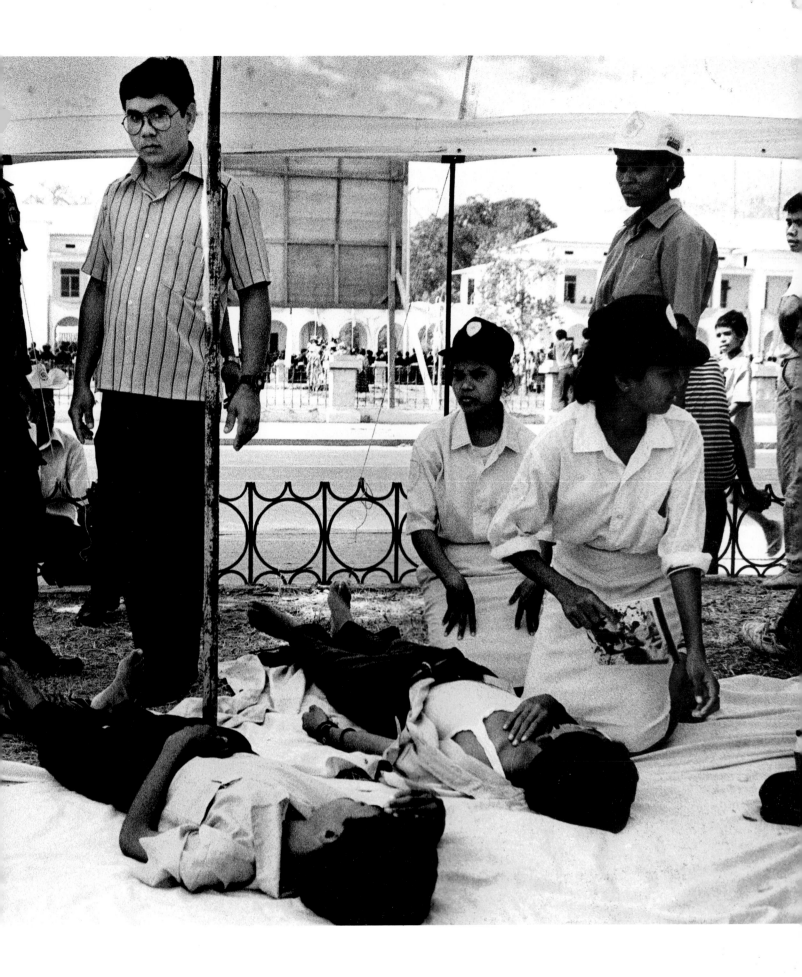

A Timorese dancer passes Indonesian soldiers on the parade ground in the front of the Governor's Residence in Dili as government officials look on.

Above Soldiers shouting and cheering on an early morning run through a suburb of Dili.

Intimidation plays a large part in the role of subjugating the population. The army marches regularly through built up areas, military check points appear and disappear overnight, so the Timorese are never sure when and where they will be stopped. Whether one lives in the capital or in a remote mountain area the oppression is inescapable; a tense atmosphere is all pervading. Many areas have military populations that outnumber the local people and it is here where some of the worst atrocities take place.

Left A street adjoining the market in Baucau. Britain supplies more military hardware to Indonesia than any other country.

Right Soldiers riding on a civilian truck on the road to Maubisse.

Snatched from his hands, an
old man has a traditional sword
examined by a soldier in Baucau.

Martial arts (*silat*) and the army in Dili.

A patrolling soldier stops at a store in Aileu.

Indonesian soldiers on an early morning march around the suburbs of Dili.

Monkeys tethered to a rope on the back of an army truck ready for transportation and sale.

Even children express fear and dread when soldiers enter their villages. Support for the men fighting in the hills comes from the population at large and many families suffer for their brothers and sisters at arms. On one occasion while walking in a back street of Dili, a young man I had met some weeks earlier approached me in a terrible state, bruised, with bloodied and torn clothing. He had been kicked and beaten by soldiers near his home twice that day, who blamed him for his father's actions in the armed resistance. He had never met his father who had taken to the hills shortly after his birth and had not been able to return home since. He had been cared for by nuns during the long periods when his mother had been imprisoned. Now reunited with his mother, barely a day passed when either of them were not subject to the unwanted attentions of the military.

Young boys waiting for soldiers to pass through the centre of Dili.

Above Military patrols instil fear into people of all ages.

Nervous children warily watch the movements of Indonesian soldiers passing through their village near Tutuala.

A climate of fear pervades life. Nervous smiles have come to symbolize East Timor; fear is so overwhelming that looking over your shoulder is instinctive. Knowing who you are talking to can sometimes be difficult. The Indonesians force people to spy or become informers through threats. Foreigners are closely watched and befriended by such people in the hope of extracting information. But the military authorities' approach is more direct. Once I was confronted by an irate officer who asked me bluntly whether I was 'gathering intelligence'. I pointed out that this was ' Visit Indonesia Year' and suggested his question seemed strange as Indonesia maintains all is well in East Timor and open to travel. 'Careless talk costs lives' has now become the maxim of every Timorese.

Men labouring in the country look over their shoulders with suspicion.

Left Security forces are positioned
at key points throughout town.
Police, keeping an eye on the
market in Baucau, make regular ID
checks.

Below A young inhabitant of Laga
eyes a stranger with suspicion.

The struggle to lead a normal life under an oppressive regime that dominates so much of your daily activity is something the Timorese have had plenty of time to come to terms with. The severe penalties for being seen with a foreigner were never enough to discourage the people from coming forward to talk about their plight. Spontaneous outpourings of emotion were accompanied by hardened resolve and words of hatred against the Indonesians. The people's wish to be independent and their dismay at the lack of action by the West, in particular Portugal, was universal. How could Kuwait be liberated and not East Timor? What made the Kuwaitis different in the eyes of the West?

Opposite A young school boy uses a fallen tree as a vantage point to watch Indonesian troops passing through the streets of Dili, October 1991.

Left Gatherings of people, unless officially sanctioned, are forbidden: even a baby's funeral is escorted by soldiers.

Above Unnatural smiles at the burial of a baby as Indonesian soldiers overshadow the grave.

Tying the spurs to a cock's legs at a cockfight in Baucau.

Below An odd situation with a man in a mask staring out of a shop front in Dili.

The first thing you notice when walking through the streets of East Timor is the shops and businesses and who owns them. It was almost impossible to find a Timorese proprietor; except in the market nearly all businesses were run by Indonesians, right down to the most humble road stall. The disparity between the two separate communities is no coincidence: as an old man explained to me on a bus trip to the east of the island, it is part of Indonesia's transmigration policy. I was surprised when he told me that, along with many of his friends, he was a labourer. After the invasion, people fled to the hills, and properties, both businesses and homes, were taken over by the Indonesians. Gradually more migrants were brought in to establish a flourishing business community. Immigrants were encouraged with incentives and opportunities to populate East Timor and the indigenous population was forced into a subservient role by the invaders. The old man had lost his job as a teacher and the only work he could get was manual labour. Educational opportunities and teaching jobs are given to the Indonesians regardless of ability and in preference to Timorese. Homes facing the sea in the former Portuguese quarter are the exclusive preserve of high-ranking Indonesians.

An old man and cockerel in the market at Baucau.

96

A young eagle for sale in Dili.

Right Becora market in Dili.

Left Another example of Indonesian benefits brought to East Timor on show in the Dili October parades. The reality is somewhat different: sanitation in most dwellings, including official establishments, is crude with open holes in the floor and cracked and overflowing pipes seeping water – that is when there isn't a water shortage.

Opposite The shortage of water and the means to extract it, has forced whole communities to dig for water wherever possible.

Rusting landing craft lie on the beaches in Dili as a reminder of the invasion. These were not the only ships to arrive off the coast of East Timor; shortly after the time of the invasion cargo vessels arrived to take away the contents of plundered houses and public buildings. Even taps and bathroom fittings turned up in hotel suites in Bali some months later.

A fisherman mends his nets with the rusting hulks of military landing craft all around.

Out of the towns and villages roads fall away and crumble on the edge of precipices. Pot holes riddle the roads from one end of the island to the other. Electricity in Dili is erratic and virtually nonexistent beyond its fringes, water is in short supply everywhere. Portuguese architecture is left to decay, and the only outward sign of any real new building seems to be of a military nature in the many complexes that dot the island. Government buildings are new, while the sewage system is crumbling; the civilian hospital is old and overcrowded and pales in comparison to the military complex. Nevertheless, the Indonesians claim that they have brought more to East Timor than the Portuguese ever did.

A baby bathes in a bucket of water.

Right A woman lies stricken with tuberculosis in an infirmary in Viqueque.

A welcoming committee to Ainaro and a guided tour by the Indonesian security services comprised of a series of walks from the police building that doubled as the one and only guest house in town, to the local *warung* (Indonesian eating house). Nervous Timorese gave side-long glances as we passed by while Indonesians grinned. Foreigners, like locals, become the objects of close scrutiny.

Above A man peers through clothing hanging between houses in Ainaro.

Right Indonesian military police quarters in Ainaro.

A visit to church during Mass would inevitably find it filled to capacity. Offering both spiritual and material support the church has been an important factor in the battle for survival. Priests and nuns have not been exempt from the harsh realities of life in East Timor and beatings and detention are not unknown. A padre recounted the time when soldiers threw rocks through his windows and fired shots over his roof until he was forced to come out and explain why he had been visiting a family who has a son in the hills. Acts of violence have been committed against every person in society regardless of position or sanctity.

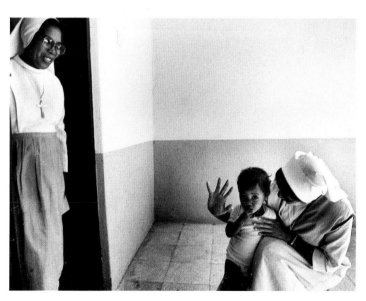

Above Timorese boys on a float participating in a church parade.

Top right When the church is full, worshippers listen to the sermon from outside.

Centre right Orphans playing basketball in front of an old Portuguese school building in Venilale.

Bottom right Many orphans of the twenty-year struggle are cared for by the church.

Closely monitored floats in a
Catholic Church parade commem-
orate the anniversary of the arrival
of Catholicism in East Timor.

Sebastião's death became a flashpoint of suppressed emotion leading up to the massacre at Santa Cruz. As the funeral cortege passed through the streets, young people shouted for freedom and independence and an end to the Indonesian occupation. On this occasion the people were not challenged by the authorities but weeks later paid a horrible price for voicing their feelings. Sebastião was killed while hiding in a church where he had fled with other young people in fear of their lives.

Left A man lays flowers on the grave of a boy shot by Indonesian soldiers in the grounds of the Motael church.

Above Mourners at the burial of a boy.

A man explains what life was like on Atauro island during a period in the late 70s when this small island, seen from the shores of Dili, acted as a vast concentration camp.

Timorese boys practising silat with a Javanese army instructor in Lospalos.

Timorese have been forced to join the Indonesian army and made to fight their own people. They are often put in the front line of a 'push' in the mountains and refusal to fight leads to execution. The Indonesian propaganda extends as far as the grave since these conscripts are buried in military cemeteries with honours to their courageous fight against the rebels.

Harvesting in an area of intense military activity.

Above and opposite Soldiers leave people in a state of terror when they pass through their towns and villages. An old man who has been beaten by the military is tended by nervous inhabitants of a small hamlet in the mountains.

Forced statements are extracted through beatings. Soldiers and police are rewarded when a person confesses to having contact with the armed resistance. People disappear or are brought in without reason for questioning, a multitude of hidden fears envelop life, visits in the dead of night and torture are commonplace and every family can recount a story of personal tragedy.

People listening to government speeches in Dili above a scene of construction.

Medical artillery: propaganda takes many strange forms including this float passing through Dili during a day of parades.

Left and below Soldiers watching the people perform in a rehearsal for the arrival of the Portuguese delegation. The special itinerary arranged by the Indonesians for the delegation involved carefully rehearsed traditional performances of song and dance at various locations on their guided tour of the island.

Offering positive images for visiting foreigners, Indonesian propaganda adorns buildings and public places. Every family was instructed to erect a flag pole outside their home and fly the Indonesian flag in anticipation of an international delegation. Accounts of Indonesian soldiers being told to wear civilian clothes and to hide military equipment from the gaze of visiting foreign dignitaries are common.

Indonesian soldiers on a truck near the airport in Baucau.

On 5 September 1991 at a checkpoint on the way out of Baucau, vehicles carrying young people of the Catholic Church (Juventude Católica de Baucau) were stopped from going to Dili where a peaceful protest would be held against integration. An Indonesian major forced the children out of the buses, threatened them with reprisals and lined them up to be photographed - another intimidatory ploy used by the authorities to instill fear and dread. His soldiers robbed them of money and valuables.

Opposite The photographer being photographed: the Indonesians like to record all.

In the months leading up to the date that was set for the arrival of the Portuguese delegation, the Indonesians increased their military presence throughout the island in an attempt to cut off communication between the armed and civil resistance and to contain Falintil (armed resistance) to the mountains. The fear of the Timorese meeting the delegation and expressing their wishes led to an all-out assault on the resistance; a campaign that included strict curfews was backed up with threats. The military authorities went to towns and villages and made announcements about the coming of the delegation and told the people that demonstrations or dialogue with the delegates would be punishable by death.

Indonesian soldiers scouring the perimeters of a village near Lospalos.

The ubiquitous military presence dominates life – army reinforcements were brought in to Dili in October 1991 to suppress the population.

Boys sleeping in Santa Cruz cemetery prior to the expected arrival of the Portuguese delegation. Fear drove many youngsters to hide in churches and cemeteries to avoid nightly searches of their homes by the military.

The young people's resistance is an enduring spirit of hope and courage. Having seen their friends and family murdered they are still prepared to come forward to make known their feelings to any foreign delegation despite the consequences. Only a matter of weeks after the 12 November massacre, young Timorese came down to the shores of Dili to meet what they had heard was a ship coming from Portugal in response to the massacre.

As these words are being written (at the end of 1994) a short news item from Associated Press reports the following: Protest Deaths – Club-wielding troops and police broke up a protest against the Indonesian military in the East Timor capital of Dili, killing three students and injuring 30, a human rights activist said.

Left Digging a grave in Maubisse. The headstone is indicative of the feeling of many families and translates 'Our yearning and sadness we bury and give our last thoughts to our sons, brothers and families'.

Opposite Boys fishing in Dili share a fleeting moment of relief.

A spear fisherman on the shore in Dili.